CU00663856

Praise for Love and Imperfection:

"For the one who helps and the one who is helped. We are always both, at the same time, though we may not realize this truth. In her beautiful, wise memoir, Clare Myatt shows us this truth and how it works.

Through her personal, poetic story of a therapist's journey to self-awareness and growth, Clare has woven a memoir of mutual help and change through the shared power of *agape* – the selfless love of one person for another without sexual implications… an experience that can create and contain a trusting, loving relational space for both people.

More than attributing change to any school of therapy, she illustrates the healing power of the therapists' self-honesty, a willingness to meet the other deeply without judgment, and an acceptance that the client's unfolding of insight and honesty will be nurtured and contained within the deep trust of this mutually open and authentic relationship – a bond paradoxically allowed by the underlying structure and practice of professional boundaries.

Clare shows us – the reader, therapist, client – that we

are all of these in one and that the deepest experiences of help and of change occur when both therapist and client have a commitment to truth and authenticity with each other.

I hope Clare's poignant and courageous book will reach countless people who will benefit beyond measure from her invitation to join her in relationship and to be changed by it."

– *Stephanie Brown Ph.D., Director, The Addictions Institute and author of 'Treating the Alcoholic: A Developmental Model of Recovery'*

* * *

"I have loved reading this book, it is a beautiful work filled with humanity and love and insight. Unassuming, subtle and gently radiant. There is rigour here too, and deep expertise, generously shared but lightly held. There are so many layers, from rich learning for therapeutic and coaching professionals, to tenderly expressed human truths which can benefit everyone. All woven through with touching stories of people's lives and loves, pain and healing. It's a genuinely rare work and a gift."

– *Francis Briers, Leadership Consultant, Executive Coach, Spiritual Counsellor and author of 'My Tao Te Ching - A Fool's Guide to Effing the Ineffable'*

* * *

"I deeply appreciate this brave book. It is a humble exposé of what the therapist usually leaves hidden behind the stage curtain. The story provides a tangible example of the work of therapy without getting lost in explanations or professional jargon. The writing style makes this book one of the most accessible and effortless accounts of the work of therapy and the life of working as a therapist that I have read. The level of transparency is inspiring, deeply honest and I can imagine many readers, whether clients, therapists, students or the general public, being touched, enlightened and relieved by the candour and insight into the world of therapy; a world that is often shrouded in mystery and kept opaque by the arrogance of professionalisation."

– *Greg Madison Ph.D., Psychologist, Psychotherapist & Focusing Coordinator, author of 'Theory and Practice of Focusing-Oriented Psychotherapy: Beyond the Talking Cure'*

* * *

"A heartwarming story about the power of love and relationship in the therapeutic healing process. Clare's honesty and self-exploration helped me understand that we are all vulnerable in this life journey, and she is one of those gifted helpers who opens the door to awareness and healing."

– *Scarlett Heinbuch Ph.D., author of 'Waking Up To Love: Our Shared-Near Death Encounter Brought Miracles, Recovery and Second Chances'*

"I loved this book. It is a profound, brave exploration of humanity in the therapeutic relationship, and the role of love and spirit in that endeavour. Clare Myatt beautifully and bravely demonstrates how that humanity contributes to the healing of others. She also dares to mention the word 'love' as a key and important aspect of this relationship. This is a profound and important book and should be read by everyone involved in helping relationships (coaches, therapists, social workers, and so on)."

– *Pete Hamill, Strozzi Institute Senior Teacher and author of 'Embodied Leadership'*

* * *

"Clare Myatt writes that 'Love changes us; lack of love changes us'. Her very readable excerpts from a personal and professional life illustrate both changes, often connecting to the recurring theme of recovery from addiction. This is a therapist's exploration and, despite the ambivalence modern therapeutic traditions may have about love, Clare sets out the significant place agape has in her work and indeed her life. To a generation preoccupied with technique, here is a wholehearted affirmation of therapy-as-living, where imperfection may still be an expression of love."

– *Alan G. Tidmarsh, Ph.D., Focusing-oriented Therapist and Supervisor*

* * *

"This is a reflective and touching story. Clare shares her personal journey of delving deeper into the emotionality that had protected her for years. Through her dedication to serve her client Bill, she discovers the delicious, yet sometimes raw and challenging world of agape – the selfless love of another.

Finding the words to reveal the depths and capacity of the human heart is beyond challenging. As a somatic coach, I am well aware that while working with certain clients, I am nudged to examine new corners of my own internal landscape. Those clients remain a special part of me. I carry forward my learnings from them with pride and gratitude. We learn from Clare's masterful job of beautifully sharing her discoveries, that which, to some is known as Spirit. To others, it is known as agape."

– *Merle McKinley, Strozzi Institute Master Somatic Coach and International Coach Federation MCC*

* * *

"From the first few pages, I was gripped. This is a beautifully honest, empathic and compassionate memoir. I'd recommend it for trauma survivors, therapists, coaches, and anyone interested in different types of trauma, shame, recovery and the potential for resilience and post traumatic growth."

– *Eve Menezes Cunningham, Past Chair of BACP Coaching and author of '365 Ways to Feel Better: Self-care Ideas for Embodied Wellbeing'*

"As writers, our most important test is to speak the truth. Clare does that in Love & Imperfection. I was immediately drawn into the story and wanted to find out more. Clare's journey through education, therapy, sobriety, and California is enlightening, and something for the curious.

So often in life, we may demure. Who me? No, I don't need any help. But, if we see another's path we may say, "Yeah, that may be the way to go." Clare's story is an easily accessible roadmap for the pathway of life."

– *Robert Golling, US Navy Retired*

* * *

"I have been fortunate enough to know and work with Clare for nearly a decade. I knew she was an exceptional therapist and supervisor and had an incredible ability to enable others to go beyond the surface into the depths that really matter. Her book both demonstrates this and takes us even further into the world of shame, in a manner that we can all bear. Clare's willingness to share herself, something therapists often avoid and to so honestly, show how her and Bill's stories intertwine, is brave and a gift to us all. I am left with so many thoughts about myself and who I am – a sign of a truly great book."

– *Keren Smedley, Executive Coach and author of 'Live the Life you Love at 50+: A Handbook for Career and Life Success'*

Love
&
Imperfection

A Therapist's Story

For Silvia,
a creative soul, courageously
finding her way.
With warmest wishes,
Clare Myatt

CLARE MYATT LLB, MA

First published in 2019 by Coaching International
With the help of Lumphanan Press
www.lumphananpress.co.uk

© Clare Myatt 2019

The author has asserted her moral right to be identified as the author of this work. All Rights reserved. No part of this publication may be reproduced, stored in a retrieval system or transmitted, in any form or by any means without the prior consent of the author, nor be otherwise circulated in any form of binding or cover other than that which it is published and without a similar condition being imposed on the subsequent purchaser.

Every possible effort has been made to ensure the accuracy of the information contained in this book and to acknowledge the sources. The publisher and author cannot accept responsibility for any errors or missions, however caused. No responsibility for loss or damage occasioned to any person acting, or reraining from action, as a result of the material in this publication can be accepted by the editor, publisher or author.

Printed & bound by ImprintDigital.com, UK

ISBN: 978-1-9160456-2-0

Dedicated to Bill, with gratitude

CONTENTS

FOREWORD

by Richard Strozzi-Heckler, Ph.D.

THIS IS A BOOK ABOUT AUTHENTICITY, INTEGRITY, and courage. It's also about the importance of including the soma in therapeutic healing, transformational work, and how we embody our values. Furthermore, it asks us to reflect deeply on what we mean by love, and how the paucity of love is the very root of so much aggression, alienation, and violence in our world. In this way it is an important book.

We live in an emotional plague. Our educational system buoyed by philosophical underpinnings that have positioned our emotional, feeling life separate and inferior to the life of concepts and thinking, has led to a fragmentation in our society and a debilitating dysfunction in our relationships. By feeling I don't mean, "have a feeling" or "express your emotions" although this may occur. I mean connecting with the deep, core energy that animates and generates our livingness. In various cultures this is called prana, elan vital, ki, chi, or life energy. When we dismiss our bodies as subordinate to rational thinking we are severely limiting our capacity for empathy, intimacy, skillful action, wisdom, pleasure, and a deeper contact with our spiritual longings.

Clare Myatt reveals how this inner dynamic of polarization can lead to a life of addiction, isolation, fear, and shame. She does this not by exposition or psychological explanations, but by her own personal journey. In a frank, lyrical style we walk along side Clare as she goes through a profound transformation with her client.

This is not one of those stylized, confessional books that have been so recently popularized, but a genuine, heartfelt journey in which many of the protocols and procedures that are part of Clare's profession are rigorously confronted. Living in a time of fake news, explicit lies, social media fabrications, and the endless striving for identity construction, this book stands out as refreshingly transparent, authentic, rigorously honest, and deeply compassionate.

Clare is an experienced licensed Marriage and Family Therapist, a somatic based psychotherapist, and a Master Somatic Coach. Her credentials are impeccable and she gives a veteran's voice to the shibboleths that have long resided in the therapeutic community; that is, *agape*, the selfless, non-sexual love that the health professional can have with their client. The honest examination of the therapeutic relationship in this book shines a bright light on the importance of the therapist or coach to be a genuine human being while embodying the ethics of the professional.

This book is a rich offering, full of wisdom and insight that can only be acquired through experience and disciplined effort. Clare's story radiates authenticity and inspiration, which make for a compelling read and plants seeds for deeper reflection on the nature of human relationships.

Richard Strozzi-Heckler, Ph.D.
Founder, Strozzi Institute

INTRODUCTION

agape (as in 'love') n.:
Selfless love of one person for another without sexual implications
(especially love that is spiritual in nature).

IT TAKES A BRAVE THERAPIST TO USE THE WORDS 'client' and 'love' in the same sentence. There is such taboo about loving our clients. It's as if we can't say 'love' without sex being implied. Yet the kind of love I'm talking about is completely distinct from the love I feel for my husband, my friends, my family.

Of all the clients I've worked with over decades of practice on both sides of the Atlantic, one stands out. His name was Bill and I loved him. Dare I say that out aloud? I wasn't *in love* with Bill, had no sexual feelings for him, no desire to spend time with him beyond the confines of the therapy room, and yet there was something special and unique about our connection.

I changed his life, and he changed mine.

Something stirred in me during the course of our work. A sense of the possibility of love and healing, not just for him, but also for me. Both shaped by decades of trauma-shame-addiction, we seemed fated to influence one another's lives in unimaginable ways. Someone very dear once said to me, 'There are people waiting for you' and I wonder if Bill and I were somehow, inexplicably, waiting for one another.

Describing what unfolded has been challenging on many levels. As confidentiality is an organising principle in my work, writing about our exchange flies in the face of all I hold dear. Yet Bill was clear; he gave his express permission to speak candidly about our work for the benefit of others following in his footsteps. And taking a leaf from his book, I lay bare my own struggle in and out of the treatment room, revealing our failures and frailties, our flawed imperfect selves.

How I wish our path had been clear, easy and successful. Not so. It was a case of two fallible human beings attempting to navigate the thorny path of building a strong sense of self without the benefit of a strong early foundation.

This book actually started its life as another one altogether. Called *Embodied Recovery*, it wove together Bill's story with those of other clients. And when I typed the final full stop I knew Bill deserved his own story and I began again.

PROLOGUE

January 2001

As memories of his time in Vietnam came to the fore, my client Bill began to talk softly and slowly about some of the scenes he was remembering and what he was feeling in his body. I listened attentively, sometimes repeating back what he said, sometimes simply nodding even though he had his eyes closed and couldn't see me, sometimes murmuring 'mmm' or 'aha' quietly. Lying on the bodywork table, his body began to shake, first arms and legs, then torso, and I both assisted and soothed.

Then something shifted. I began to feel nauseous and faint. Not just a little, but overwhelmingly sick, as if I was going to throw up if I didn't lose consciousness first. The room swam. I staggered back against the wall for support and could feel incredible heat surge through my body. I felt scared and inadequate. While I was concerned for my own wellbeing, I was far more concerned for Bill's. I couldn't leave him in this state and yet I had diminishing capacity to stay and be with him. I hoped and prayed that what I was feeling would pass, that it would simply be a wave of something weird moving through and I would recover. And then he said, 'Are you there? Can you smell that?'

And I could. There was an eerie odour hanging in the room. I can't tell you what it smelled like because I've no idea what it was. Perhaps it was the smell of death in Vietnam. Perhaps it was Agent Orange, or napalm, or bodies burning, or... I honestly have no words other than a sense of being in the presence of evil. I felt insufficient for the task at hand. I held on to the wall in the vague hope I wouldn't drown in whatever toxicity was filling the room. The shocking odour seemed to be emanating from Bill's body, not like perspiration, more like foul steam rising from a swamp. I grounded through my feet, breathed as best I could, tried to keep my head above the waves. Time stood still, appallingly so. I was afraid of drowning.

I don't know how much time passed. And then I heard Bill begin to pray. I don't know what he said. I couldn't hear his words clearly, but it was as if a miracle was unfolding, as if angels or some unfathomable spiritual presence was holding back the evil and dissolving it. The odour diminished, everything settled, space opened up. Bill became quiet and peaceful; I settled as well. *There were no words*. Nothing useful to say about this incredible experience we'd shared.

Eventually he sat up and slowly sipped a glass of water. He looked a decade younger and somehow both relieved and tired all at once. He simply smiled, nodded, and with tears in his eyes took his leave. *There were still no words*.

Never before had my deep resources deserted me. Nor have they since. The experience cemented a belief in me that this is the work I'm supposed to do, that I was merely a conduit for something greater than me, and I felt honoured, humbled and deeply grateful.

Seventeen Years Later

I've often reflected on this experience. It's only now, with the benefit of hindsight and experience, that other words come to mind as well: surrender, faith, love, hope, trust, grace, intuition, divine guidance.

> And now abides faith, hope, love, these three; but the greatest of these is love.

CHAPTER ONE

Meeting Bill

TOWARDS THE END OF DECEMBER 1999 I CHECKED
my messages after morning client sessions, and listened
to the soft and halting voice of someone who didn't even
leave his name, just a request to call back. My curiosity
piqued, I made the call. The still unnamed male answered.
He said he'd been referred by a mutual friend, Morrie
Frappier, someone I'd served with as Home Counsellor
for San Luis Obispo (SLO) County's Child Protective
Services where we had both been collecting hours of
supervised experience towards Marriage and Family
Therapy (MFT) licensure in California. I remembered
we had alcoholism recovery in common and immediately
wondered if this gentleman had a similar concern. I
asked the usual questions – what kind of things did he

want to talk about, when was he available, was my fee affordable, and did he have any questions for me? There was a hesitation.

'Well,' he said, wavering 'I got some pretty tough things to talk about, kinda wondering if you think you can handle that? You sound like a nice young lady and maybe I'm too much for you?'

I smiled. I paused as well. 'Shall we wait and see? Come on in and let's meet first, then you can decide.' He agreed and we arranged an appointment for later that week.

I wondered who I'd be meeting. From the sound of his voice I thought he was probably older than me, weighed down, perhaps lonely, and pondered the nature of the 'tough things' he mentioned. When we met what took me by surprise was the sweetness of his demeanour, the gentle energy as he took my hand to shake our introduction of hello. Not only that, but his appearance. It wasn't often I encountered a man in well-laundered denim work overalls – rare was the traditional bib and brace outfit worn at that time (however much it became a fashion statement later on). Greying hair curled over his collar and a shaggy beard adorned his face, drawing attention to the blue eyes above – dimmed with tiredness yet warm and tender. All in contrast to the tough stuff he seemed so concerned about.

Shaking hands, he said, 'Pleased to meet you, ma'am,

my name is Bill.' I felt the hard-working leather of his palm against mine, and made eye contact, feeling cautiously welcomed an inch into his world. Stepping deeper into the consulting room, I patted the arm of the chair across from mine to suggest where to land; we both sat down and I allowed him time to look around and drink in his surroundings.

As he sat across from me, smiling softly yet with such pain and sadness in his eyes, I noticed he folded his hands in his lap to camouflage their slight tremor. I wondered about DT's (delirium tremens, hands shaking due to alcohol withdrawal); then I wondered if there was some neurological cause for the almost imperceptible movement; and I settled, for now, on the cause being anxiety. He was unfamiliar with female company and my gentle attentiveness perturbed him

'So, Bill' I began, proceeding with caution into ice-breaking territory before plunging into the deeper waters of working agreements and the way ahead, 'Morrie has referred you. How do you guys know one another?'

'He used to be my counsellor. He understands the alcohol stuff.' After a pause, he looked up from the floor, making momentary eye contact as he continued. 'He said you'd understand.'

Much was exchanged in the richness of that momentary eye contact; almost more than words can say. There was a deep connection and a resonance. Almost no need to nod and acknowledge my own familiarity with alcohol. In that moment I decided to reveal my own decade of sobriety. A glint of acknowledgement showed in his eyes and he nodded.

I had so many questions, and I sensed he needed lots of space and time in which to answer the key ones. Here was someone who was already judging himself so harshly that any sniff of judgement from me would do harm. I needed to build trust – slowly, carefully, diligently and respectfully. This I could do. Actually, enjoyed doing. I knew how it felt to be held, metaphorically speaking, by the soft attention of a therapist, having had any number myself over the past couple of decades. I started by asking what had brought him to therapy – why me? Why now?

His body relaxed and he replied, 'Morrie and me, we want to go sailing together. He doesn't have a boat right now, so we could go on mine at the weekends sometimes. We have this plan.' He smiled cautiously, just revealing the edges of his teeth beneath a fringe of moustache. 'We want to sail to Hawaii, both love it there. But he's sober and I want to be to make the trip, only right, and 'cos we're buds he can't be my counsellor, so I need someone else. That's why I'm here. He recommended you. Like I said, he said you'd understand.'

Bill's previous experience in counselling made it easier to get under way, so after reviewing my working agreement, we started by exploring his family of origin.

Being trained as a Bowenian systems therapist, I prefer to begin by drawing a genogram (family tree) so that I can understand how my client has been shaped from their earliest times. I knew we were going to be exploring his relationship to alcohol. Understanding its role in his family, its influence on him growing up and currently would be enormously informative. I asked if we could start there and he agreed.

'Hawaii' he said simply. 'Born there. Love it, that's why we want to sail to The Big Island.' Then, as if a cloud passed over the sun, he paused. 'But the beginning was bad. Started off as a haole.' I had no idea what this word meant (pronounced 'howlie'), so I had to ask. 'It's what the natives call us whites. It ain't good.' He looked down, away, broke contact. I wondered if this was the tough stuff. 'I ran away' he blurted out. 'I was terrified and I ran away.' His eyes filled with tears. I had no idea we would be in such tender territory so quickly.

We needed to back up, slow it down, go back to the beginning. For the remainder of this first session and the next, Bill gradually filled in the detail of his life. It was quite a story. He was born in 1947, the second of four children, his father a functioning alcoholic and his mother an elementary school teacher of Danish heritage, her father coming from a strict military background. The children were each two years apart, Bill now fifty-two. Growing up in Hawaii was both heaven and hell. The divine weather, beaches to explore, ocean to play in, freedom to run pretty wild with his younger brother ran counter to the hellish experience at home – an unpredictably intoxicated Dad, strict Mom, and then there was school and the whole 'haole' experience.

Between sessions I did some research on this, as 'haole' was new to me. Apparently it's a term used by native Hawaiians to describe anyone born beyond their shores and settling there, predating even Captain Cook's arrival in 1778. In short, a word to describe intruders. While there is disagreement about its exact origins, I rather liked the interpretation related to the breath. When Hawaiians greet one another, touching noses and inhaling together, they actually share the same breath. Europeans by contrast did no such thing, perhaps shaking hands instead, so foreigners were described as being breathless, the word 'haole' literally meaning 'no breath'. The implication went deeper – not only without-breath but also without spirit – so important in these Polynesian isles with such a deep spiritual tradition.

Bill described his childhood as confusing. Times of elation running free in paradise contrasted with times of terror, sometimes at home and more often bullied at school. We came full circle to the incident which created so much distress for him. One day he was walking home from school with his younger brother and they were ambushed by a group of slightly older Hawaiian boys from their school. Bill knew he needed to be tough, stand up to them for the sake of his dignity and certainly to protect Jimmy, a mere eight years old at the time. But he was terrified. And in that fight or flight moment – when we are not in charge of our responses, when our autonomic nervous system takes over to protect us as best it knows how – he ran. Jimmy got quite a beating. If that weren't bad enough, Bill got his own beating from Dad for being a coward.

There are moments when whole lives can be shaped. This was one of those moments. There would, of course, be more.

Already cowed by the unpredictable nature of his father's moods and drunkenness, not knowing from one day to the next if home would be safe, Bill's sensitivity had him at the mercy of each new trauma. Horrified at his natural instinct to flee rather than face down the bullies, he decided everything he'd been hearing from his father over the years was true. 'You're nothing and you're never gonna amount to nothing' is what he heard relentlessly from Dad. Sometimes the power of the ocean would push back and he'd hear a small voice in his head saying, 'No, no, don't listen, you're bold and brave, you're okay.' He felt a failure. He had failed to protect his brother. He'd failed his brother, himself, his father, his mother, his siblings, he really was nothing and no-one. A nobody and a coward.

Even writing this now has me pause and take a deep breath. I remember thinking at the time that we had a lot of work to do. Yet there was more! In the very next session I learned that he'd done two tours of duty in Vietnam and been treated for alcoholism soon thereafter, cancer two decades later. Here was a man with his very own Four Horsemen of the Apocalypse – not the biblical ones – instead, Shame, Trauma, Alcoholism, Cancer.

Shame

While guilt reflects feeling bad about something we've done, shame reflects feeling bad about who we are. It's a *being* fault rather than a *doing* fault.

A multitude of influences shaped Bill's relationship to shame. We all grow up with a deep desire to feel loved, accepted and belong. No matter how hard Bill strived in his family, the particular character structures of his parents made this difficult – his father's alcoholism, his mother's military-level precision and discipline. Whatever he did, it wasn't good enough, and it is this enduring experience which creates internalised shame.

Bill's innate sensitivity exacerbated this sense of shame. Those shaming remarks did not land on teflon and slide off; they were absorbed deep into his being. As one of the roughly twenty per cent of the population dubbed a 'Highly Sensitive Person' by researcher Dr. Elaine Aron,[1]

Bill experienced and processed everything deeply. It was as if he were defending against a cruel world without skin for protection.

Another powerful layer was his experience in the wider culture as a *haole* – in the hierarchy of Hawaii, he felt at the bottom, a white immigrant being the lowest of the low. He was bullied by locals at school, and as we've already heard, found himself unable to defend his younger brother on that fateful day. Identifying as a coward, he internalised a deep self-loathing, another facet of shame.

School was a particular contributor. Beyond bullying, academic subjects became problematic. A straight 'A' student to start with, experience with a new teacher part-way through second-grade shifted results to failing 'F's, and by the time he was twelve years old Bill could no longer see the board due to poor eyesight – he was too embarrassed to ask for help and didn't get glasses until ninth grade. The advent of specs intensified the bullying and he sought solace in the escapism of science fiction. Able to see at last, he became an avid reader from then on, sci-fi always a comfort.

Trauma

When I talk to clients about trauma I describe two horizontal scales. One measures trauma – from small 't' trauma at one end to capital 'T' Trauma at the other. The other measures sensitivity – from small 's' sensitivity at one end to capital 'S' Sensitivity at the other.

Suppose someone experiences a small 't' trauma (say falling off their bike the first time stabilisers come off). If they have other successes to draw on, are well-resourced, and have low level sensitivity, then this event may not even register or be memorable for more than a few hours. If, however, they have high-level sensitivity then this small 't' trauma begins to move up the scale to something more noteworthy. The higher the sensitivity, the more significant becomes the trauma, its effects and consequences, and the more likely someone will develop Post Traumatic Stress Disorder or PTSD.

We already knew Bill was sensitive. He knew it in his bones and had been told as much since day one. His father saying, 'You're such a sissy, so f***ing sensitive' simply affirmed what he already knew to be true. He preferred being alone to having company; being outside in natural wide-open spaces with not another soul in sight was one of his joys. He hated those supermarkets piled high with vivid boxes, accompanying bright lights, bouncy music, people rushing up and down the aisles with trolleys; a nightmare. Bill could empathically dip into someone else's experience and know how they felt, intuiting as easily as breathing. A deeply sensitive soul.

His father's harsh words, his mother's discipline, the untenable environment at school – words and experiences didn't land on the surface, they somehow burrowed deep inside, wounding like a warm knife cuts through butter. Layered onto this unpromising start were his traumatic experiences in Vietnam, reinforced by the medical trauma surrounding the cancer diagnosis. Significant trauma over a lifetime. A straightforward diagnosis of PTSD[2] was easy to reach.

Bill wasn't alone. The National Vietnam Veterans Readjustment Study (1990) reports a PTSD incidence of 30.9% for men and 26.9% for women Vietnam veterans.[3]

PTSD dogged Bill's existence every single day. He *re-experienced* his Vietnam experience through flash-backs, both day and night. He routinely experienced nightmares and 'night terrors'. He was loathe to describe them in detail, preferring to forget them as best he could. And yet, they were the primary reason he gave for not being successful in relationship. He couldn't bear the thought of anyone being with him when he awoke shouting, sweating and thrashing amongst the bedclothes. His daytime flashbacks could be triggered by something in the environment – like the crack of a car backfiring sounding similar to a gunshot – and sometimes by something internal, such as the fear of being lost and alone.

Bill's *intrusive thoughts* came unbidden either out of the blue or in relation to something more tangible. For example, he could be in a business meeting, managing the background anxiety well enough, and suddenly experience critical parental voices in his head. Able to stay physically in the room, aware of the context of the meeting and those present, he could even continue to engage in the conversation, yet his internal landscape would be peopled by voices from the past intruding on the present. This is a different experience from a flash-back – here someone feels as if they are back in a different time and place, disconnected from the present, having difficulty functioning in real time.

Another classic PTSD symptom involves *avoidance* – people, places or things bringing back memories. Over time, the list of things that reminded him of Vietnam diminished, yet there remained a whole host of circum-stances which could pitch him back there in an instant: heat and humidity, sweat trickling down his back, tasting some foods, brackish warm water, vehicles backfiring, certain odours, memorabilia, movies, letters from those times, media coverage of Vietnam or current conflicts, military uniforms and so on. Avoiding his comrades-in-arms was easy. He cut off contact with them all; it was simply too painful. While some veterans find great solace in writing about their experiences, reminiscing with buddies, staying in touch with what passed before, Bill sought the opposite.

Fundamentally, Bill was scared by intense emotions and avoided them whenever possible. He wanted 'happy' and avoided 'joy'; he felt 'irritated' and avoided 'angry'. Alcohol was a particular ally here as it levelled all the emotions into vaguer, woollier, swirling pastels rather than bold bright colours.

Along with many of his comrades, Bill was often overwhelmed by strong feelings of guilt, hopelessness and shame. He felt guilty about what he'd done in Vietnam, despite everything; he certainly felt shame about not only his experience there, having survived it when so many did not, but also in relation to life events prior to the draft. And hopelessness? There were sober times when he could rise above the slough of despondence, even be cheerful and have hope for the future, yet there were other times, particularly when he was drinking, that hopelessness was his constant companion.

A classic component of depression, anhedonia (loss of joy in things previously found rewarding) was less of an issue for Bill when he was sober, increasing in direct correlation with alcohol consumption. One thing sustained him – his love of the ocean and his boat. He felt more connected to his Higher Power on board a ship than at any other time, and this was a great comfort.

While Bill managed to keep a lid on the majority of his irritability and anger during our sessions, he told me of times when he'd been unable to do so in public, humiliating himself or others in the process. He described fear as background music – always there, sometimes louder, sometimes quieter – rarely without volume at all. He still managed to achieve courageous things in the face of fear, yet gave himself little credit. That he'd established and ran a successful engineering company did nothing for his self-esteem.

Alcoholism

The classic definition of an alcoholic[4] is someone who drinks alcohol, suffers negative consequences (great or small), and despite those negative consequences, continues to drink. Drinking becomes a compulsive behaviour that increasingly consumes thought patterns and actions over time. A non-alcoholic organises their life around what they care about – health, relationships, work, interests, fun and so on; an alcoholic organises their life around alcohol – thinking about it, planning where and when to buy it, where to drink it, where to get more of it. Alcohol becomes the dominant organising principle.

Bill didn't use alcohol in adolescence as many do; instead he began to drink in Vietnam to numb deep discomfort and distress. It worked like a charm. His father's son, he was already genetically pre-disposed to become alcoholic rather than be able to drink on a take-it or leave-it basis. Once he started, he was on a slippery slope not of his own making. The haze of alcohol intoxication managed so much – the fear of not belonging in this bizarre environment, numbing the pain, helping him forget and get to sleep, assuaging the night terrors in some small way. Bill also experienced the customary blackouts – where the brain seems not to record events, instead providing either still photos or brief video-clips of what has passed, whole swathes of time being lost. This was both a relief and further fuel for shame. What had happened? Layers of *couldn't remember* and *didn't know*.

Much has been written about the overlap between trauma and self-medicating with alcohol or other drugs. It really is a perfect marriage. Trauma evokes intolerable feelings, alcohol numbs those feelings – at least for a while – then the cycle starts all over again to become a runaway train hurtling down the track towards potential disaster.

Cancer

Bill was diagnosed with cancer in his forties. Under 'current health' on his intake form he wrote 'colostomy from colon cancer but this is not really a problem' and aside from acknowledging embarrassment in the face of intimacy, he rarely referred to the diagnosis. I found this quite remarkable on many levels as it could have been grounds for bitterness, hopelessness, anxiety, fear and sadness, to say nothing of fuelling PTSD and alcoholism.

The Veterans Administration acknowledges a link between cancer and exposure to ionizing radiation and Agent Orange.[5] Given the lack of other risk factors, apart from alcohol (diet, smoking, lack of physical activity, family history of colon cancer, race, diabetes, obesity), it seems most likely that time in Vietnam was responsible for Bill's cancer. Yet I never once heard an angry word in that direction. And while many would experience the diagnosis itself, invasive surgery and treatment there-after as traumatic, it didn't seem to add to the PTSD burden. Or perhaps he was in denial? Perhaps we *both* were? At that stage in my career I'd had little experience with clients, friends or family having cancer and, with the benefit of hindsight, can see how infrequently I ad-dressed this major underlying health concern. I wonder how much his unconscious sense of a shortened life contributed to drinking? After all, he knew he was going to die sooner rather than later, so why not soothe the path into oblivion?

* * *

Bill's Four Horsemen of the Apocalypse – Shame, Trauma, Alcoholism, Cancer – defined his life, some more, some less. What follows is an honest recounting of our work together, based on notes and recordings. But first, I want to relate something of the therapist he found to work with. What was I bringing beyond my professional expertise?

CHAPTER TWO

Numbing with Alcohol

Altered States

Sometime in 1980, soon after starting a law degree in Nottingham, I went with friends to see the Ken Russell movie *Altered States*. William Hurt played a Harvard scientist who conducted experiments on himself involving a hallucinatory drug in an isolation chamber, potentially causing genetic regression. I can recall, even now, his arms rippling as if snakes were pushing their way around underneath the skin and I began to cry. No-one else did. And I cried consistently throughout the remainder of the movie. No-one else cried a single tear. Feeling both troubled and baffled, I figured this experience was significant and took myself off to the college counsellor. His name was Dr.

Norman Ford. A gentle soul, he'd been trained in Freud's analytical style and many a session passed without a word exchanged, simply fifty minutes of crying. In retrospect, this was far from useful, but at the time I had no way to know a nurturing presence would have been more healing. However, what *was* enormously useful was the experience of someone actually paying attention and being with me in a meaningful way, perhaps for the first time in my life. My parents' ability had been sadly lacking, grandparents much the same, and apart from a dance teacher I adored and a kindergarten teacher who wore the softest, fluffiest most delicious angora jumpers for me to snuggle into, there had not been much opportunity for me to experience attentive soothing.

Dr. Ford did what he knew to do and I did the same. I continued to use alcohol. My best friend, it took the edge off loneliness, aided sleep, reduced social inhibitions and managed the horror of sexual encounters. For college meant all of these things. Away from home for the first time, an overwhelming sense of freedom and possibility prevailed – yet, I had few tools to navigate all these exciting new experiences. Aside from family law and criminology, my studies were quite dull and I spent most of my time figuring out how to be in a relationship with others – until then I'd only ever lived with Mum and Dad, and they seemed so, well, *elderly*. Anyway, they were my parents. Suddenly I had halls of residence and what seemed like loads of young women to be around, then a flat-mate after halls became intolerable, and eventually a flat-mate and her live-in boyfriend. It was all so complicated and overwhelming.

And there were men. Lots of them. Cute ones, young ones, older ones, athletic ones, intellectual ones and my favourite type – the ones who liked to drink and pay attention to me. I was a light-weight by comparison, could hardly tolerate more than a few glasses, but I liked the melting away of my usual uptightness and constriction to be a certain 'proper' way, enjoyed the relaxation of it all.

We're talking about the Eighties – a time of big hair, shoulder-pads, pre-HIV awareness, Madonna's 'Like a Virgin' and Michael Jackson's moonwalk, *Seinfeld* and *Dallas* popular on TV. A different time. People drove drunk, had unprotected sex, smoked in pubs and restaurants in the UK. There were marijuana-infused-brownies as well as pot to smoke, and while other chemicals were available, none crossed my path. I was quite satisfied with alcohol, I wasn't looking for anything else. (For which, I have to say in retrospect, I'm enormously grateful as I'm quite sure I'd have become addicted overnight to any other substance coming my way).

Moving to America

Fast forward eight alcohol-and-drama filled years. I had an epiphany shortly before my thirtieth birthday and decided to make a big change. My choices seemed to be: (a) move to London, (b) study for a graduate degree or (c) move to the USA. I chose the latter. Initially to Dallas, then with my psychopath boss (I kid you not) to Nashville and Philadelphia. I finally escaped his clutches by moving to California. There I found a fabulous therapist, Dr Sheryn T. Scott. Endowed with exactly the qualities required for the deep reparative work I needed, she helped me begin healing the lack-of-attachment issues from childhood. One brave day I said to her, 'I think I'd like to do what you do.' Being wise, she recommended I sign up for a class before committing to a master's degree in Marriage and Family Therapy. And what did I choose? 'Chemical Dependency.' While I didn't know at the time, this was certainly no coincidence, and serendipitous for many reasons.

The first class fell on a Tuesday evening in mid-October. Brenda Underhill, then Executive Director of the Alcoholism Center for Women in Los Angeles, began by defining female alcoholism. I heard her describe me. I was dumbfounded. How could she know? How could this complete stranger know so much about me and my life? I heard her highlight the contributory factors of having a difficult childhood, with or without trauma (and by now I knew I had the full complement), sensitivity, shame, desire to escape or numb or both, alcohol as best friend, as social grease, as means of connecting sexually or otherwise. And perhaps its greatest gift? As an alcoholic I experienced blackouts. Oh, the mixed joy of not being able to remember, and the indignity of having to call someone the next day to ask, 'What happened? Did I embarrass myself? Are we still friends?' and so on. Yet the not remembering, apart from occasional freeze-frames, was gratefully welcomed. What a relief. A sense of shameful behaviour endured, yet the details were in blurry shadow, so much easier to tolerate than if they were brightly defined.

With this in mind, I approached a Kenny G concert at Universal Studios Amphitheater the following Friday with trepidation. I was going with a friend from work, one of the sales team. A fellow Brit in a sea of Americans in Los Angeles, he was married with a family and a really nice guy whose company I enjoyed. Naively, I hadn't put two and two together – why were we going alone? Sounded suspiciously like a date. Oh well, tickets bought, happy hour under way at the local bar, I specifically asked for Coke rather than my usual G&T. It wasn't until I got up to walk to the loo that I realised he'd clearly been spiking my drinks with vodka as I was completely squiffy and it was only six o'clock. The remainder of the evening escapes me – I have only a few of those blackout type photos in my mind – stumbling up the stairs at the Amphitheater trying to find my seat; wishing I hadn't worn heels; hearing him on the phone to his wife later on saying he had to stay over to close some deal or other in San Diego the following day. A Saturday? Yeah, right. When I woke up the next morning, not knowing what had happened between us overnight, I had one of those golden aha moments. *If I hadn't been under the influence, none of this would have happened.* Finally, with that clarity, I saw the consequence of my drinking (albeit foisted upon me this time) and I knew there were other choices possible, that a different life was possible. That was my last drink.

Homework from the Chemical Dependency course required attendance at a variety of the self-help twelve-step meetings available (such as Alcoholics Anonymous, Adult Children of Alcoholics, Co-dependents Anonymous and Survivors of Incest Anonymous). Twelve-step programmes have always welcomed visitors as part of their tradition to attract rather than promote. I began with AA (Alcoholics Anonymous) and attended what turned out to be a small, extremely intimate meeting across the street from my office in Glendale. I apologised, saying I was there on assignment, not for myself and if they felt uncomfortable, I would be happy to choose another meeting. I'm sure they saw through my discomfort and knew I was in exactly the right place. I was bewildered. Some of the stories I heard seemed so similar to mine – the powerlessness, the shame, how alcohol made things both easier and more difficult – yet much was so different and hard to identify with. I came away baffled and confused. While I felt clear that alcohol had no place in my life, I wasn't ready to acknowledge I was an alcoholic, and certainly felt superior to these grateful members of AA. I wasn't ready to join them. I can smile gently at that old self now, be compassionate towards the young woman for whom layers of denial and shame had yet to peel away.

Sober and Struggling

Six months into my masters degree, it was clear that I wasn't coping well at all. Sleep was problematic, I was utterly depressed, romantic relationships continued to be a disaster (married men, separated or not, a specialty). My therapist and I decided anti-depressant medication might be in order and I saw my first psychiatrist. This was a time when Prozac had just hit the market and for a while it shifted my mood most helpfully. When it stopped working it was like going over the edge of a cliff, and I was pitched into even worse depression. Endless experiments of various anti-depressants followed; suffice it to say the ensuing several years were nightmarish in terms of managing and stabilising mood. I may have been sober, officially a 'recovering alcoholic', but life was not much fun. Nor did I really know *how* to have fun – the notion of play had not been encouraged in my family. Play was considered a waste of time, with productivity and perfection being the order of the day.

One of my first therapeutic assignments will undoubtedly amuse you – 'Go to the beach, build a sandcastle and be sure to get sand underneath your fingernails!' As someone castigated in childhood for being even slightly dirty or messy, especially in the nail department, this was a big ask and I didn't enjoy it one bit. Another, some years later, was to limit movie attendance to those with an upbeat, inspiring or humorous theme. This was an even bigger ask, and I pretty much ignored the suggestion for decades. At the time, I was seeing at least a couple of movies a week, mostly art-house and foreign (to the US) and I especially loved the tragedies that were *Titanic, Endless Love, Jude, Leaving Las Vegas, Philadelphia, What's Eating Gilbert Grape...* see what I mean? Not exactly *Austin Powers* meets *Mrs. Doubtfire*.

As time passed, I knew I needed more help than my therapist alone could offer so we designed an all-encompassing programme of recovery to enhance the quality of my sober life, including healing the trauma, shame and depression that underpinned it. I engaged increasingly with other sober folk, both in and out of twelve-step meetings; let go of friends and drinking buddies from the past, however well-intentioned; engaged a personal trainer at the gym to improve my level of fitness who in turn referred me to a nutritionist for advice on healthier eating choices; took time away from work to relax and have fun; started attending a non-denominational church to explore non-Church of England possibilities for spirituality; and, finally, decided on a period of singledom to examine the appalling partner choices I had made. My therapist recommended attending a Harville Hendrix *Keeping the Love You Find* weekend workshop run locally in Pasadena, designed to uncover the childhood patterns that created such catastrophic adult partnership choices. Valuable and revealing, I determined to stay single a while longer – thus far, sobriety hadn't exactly resulted in the healthier choices I'd anticipated.

I remember one particular occasion when I was in a meeting, at that stage about five years sober. I had one of those sizzling-eye-contact moments with a dishy guy across the room and we held each other's gaze for ridic-ulously long moments over the course of the evening. I managed to arrange an introduction and discovered, to my absolute horror, that he was just a few days sober. As addic-tions specialist Terry Gorski suggests, 'When your gonads go off, run don't walk.' I may have been in recovery, but my old patterns of attraction to the emotionally unavailable remained intact.

Transformation Begins

The 1990s found me working hard towards licensure as a Marriage and Family Therapist in California – gathering the three thousand hours of supervised experience required to apply for the written and oral exams. Three thousand turned into five thousand due to a technicality in the paperwork and I worked relentlessly on, eventually passing both exams first time. Mid-November 1995 I was awarded the precious licence. I tore home from my Cambria PO box with the priceless letter-sized envelope, opened it in the kitchen with shaking hands, and let out such a scream of joy that my poor cats scattered in all directions, scared for their lives I'm sure. What an achievement! Eight years sober, licensed as a psychotherapist, ready to take on the world of private practice and beyond. Time to celebrate. Not with alcohol, though. With calls to friends awaiting their own licences and a veritable dance for joy in the living room.

Armed with my MFT licence I could now open an office to see private practice clients and I felt ill-equipped, so I enrolled in a business development course in the San Francicso Bay Area to acquire the requisite skills. Here I was exposed to ontological coaching for the first time – the work of Fernando Flores, Terry Winograd and Chilean biologists Humberto Maturana and Francisco Varela. Horizons opened wider than I expected and I met some notable people, perhaps the most influential being Dr. Richard Strozzi-Heckler.

The first time I saw him, Richard was dressed in aikido attire – white crossover *gi* on top and black wide legged pants called *hakama* below. He stood in readiness, with three others similarly dressed, poised to attack him simultaneously in what's called a *randori*. He handled them with ease, grace and dignity. I watched, mesmerised. One of those seminal moments forever stored as a bright, clear moving image. This man had something I wanted very much – a deeply centred presence inspiring confidence, calm and safety. I wanted this for myself, and I wanted to provide this for others. For the first time in as long as I could remember, I felt hopeful – here was my path, and a teacher to show me the way.

Fortuitously, a mutual friend was already studying with Richard at Strozzi Institute in Petaluma, set in the beautiful rolling country of Sonoma County about an hour north of San Francisco. I signed up for the next available training, an eighteen-day course running throughout 1998 called *Somatics in Action*. Starting here, and through the multiple courses and years that followed, healing and transformation accelerated beyond my wildest imagination.

At Strozzi Institute there was nowhere to hide. And I did love to hide. Stay invisible and narrow and make no waves – remember, be seen and not heard? They affectionately nicknamed me The Mouse. I dressed in black, long dark hair hiding most of my face, speaking only when spoken to, watching, observing, curious *all* of the time about everyone else. I carefully chose where to sit in the circle. Always opposite Richard. For that way I could keep him in view and keep myself safe. I wasn't exactly scared of him but held a very healthy respect. He could be gentle but I also knew he could bite, and bite hard. I wanted him to like me. I wanted to be special; the perfect set- up to continue healing, he became a kind of super-parent onto whom I could project every doubt, fear and outrage. I wasn't the first, and certainly wouldn't be the last to do so. He had the capacity to hold us all.

Many seminal moments ensued, some gentle, some hair-raising.

I experienced my first somatic bodywork session early on. I lay down on a massage table, fully clothed, and Deborah invited me to breath rhythmically while she touched various pressure points around the body with experienced, gentle hands. Within minutes I was cast back in time, gagging and retching as I fought to escape my grandfather. My body convulsed and rippled on the table. There was no time to think or try to be perfect, just safe space to explore what might have been possible had the resources and power of an adult been available to me then. It was all very messy and alarming, yet when I stood at the end of our session I felt transformed. A grown-up, a woman of substance and power who had endured the trauma, survived the abuse, and was equipping herself with skills to relate in new and meaningful ways. I was amazed. I'd spent so many years in traditional talk therapy – with limited results – and here was I, bursting open like a ripe seedpod with this alternative intervention. I couldn't wait to get back on the table! And get back on the table I did, repeatedly, with Deborah and other skilled practitioners in the years to come. As I said, no place to hide.

Transformation Continues

Undertaking transformational work before the turn of the twenty-first century meant trusting the process rather than relying on the evidence neuroscience has since revealed. At the time, all the evidence I needed was Richard's centred presence, so striking in the randori. His ability to listen calmly, deeply, making me feel moment to moment as if I were the only person that mattered was incredible, like nothing I'd ever known before. And he was able to produce that experience for others, not just for me, so I felt sure I wasn't mistaken. He didn't just *talk* about how to develop an embodied presence, he demonstrated how to have one and engaged us in activities to expand both capacity and competency.[6]

One of the first things we learned at Strozzi Institute

was grounding and centring. Practiced over time, this competency becomes embodied so that it can be accessed when under pressure – however much we hope to rise to the occasion 'We don't rise to the level of our expectations, we fall to the level of our training.'[7] Originating in the martial arts tradition, grounding and centring allows a measured response beyond the unstoppable autonomic nervous system's reaction under pressure: fight, flight, freeze or fold.

One beautiful sunny day in California I set off for my daily walk on the beach, unaware of this possibility. I loved being close to the ocean, hearing the waves lapping on the Cambria beach, an idyllic community midway between San Francisco in the north and Los Angeles in the south, near Hearst Castle. Strolling along, revelling in the smell of the salty air and warmth of the sun on my face, I noticed people ahead of me on the beach. I registered a dog bounding towards me and assumed he was friendly and wanted to play. *Wrong.* As the dog came alongside to my left I felt a sharp stab of pain and, time slowing to a standstill, I realised he'd bitten into my thigh. I was rooted to the spot. Totally unable to move or respond. My next awareness was another sharp stab on my right; he'd returned, running behind me and taking a chunk out of my other thigh. By this time the owner realised there was a problem and was chasing him down, brandishing a lead in his hands. He managed to secure both dogs and came over to see if I was all right. I didn't know. Clearly I was shaken, rendered speechless. He pointed to the blood running down both my legs and asked if I needed help. I was unaccustomed to noticing I needed help, asking for it, or indeed accepting it. I politely declined (at least I'm sure I did, after all that's how I was brought up) and staggered the hundred or so yards to my home. I was flabbergasted. I drove myself to the doctor's surgery and got stitched up.

The kindly doc enquired what had happened and if I'd managed to kick the dog. 'Kick the dog?!' I exclaimed. 'But that would have hurt him!'

'Er, yeah,' he responded, smiling, with a hint of sarcasm, and then we both laughed at the absurdity of it all. In that moment I learned a lot about who I am under pressure. I freeze. Most likely disassociate as well. I had had zero ability to respond to the dog's attack. I simply reacted in accordance with the natural ability we all have in our autonomic nervous system. We tend to fight, flight, freeze or fold. I definitely freeze.

Would it be useful to have greater capacity in these circumstances? Indeed it would. It's important to have that automatic survival instinct. It's not about training that out, it's about being initially triggered into fight, flight, freeze or fold and then having the capacity to respond with something else, opening up our ability to take care of the circumstances appropriately. I can't ever imagine kicking that dog, but it would have been useful to call out to the owner sooner, or move to protect myself, rather than be attacked again.

And this is not just about dogs on a beach. This is about all kinds of routine experiences in our day-to-day lives. It's the moment when the boss comes in and says, 'I'd like to see you in my office'; or we hear an internalised critical voice saying, 'You're hopeless, it's hopeless, give up'; or the train's late and we're worried about missing a meeting; or the phone rings and we see someone's name appear on the screen we'd rather not talk to; or someone says, 'What would you like for dinner?' and we're lost for words even though we'd really prefer Italian to Chinese. In the myriad moments when we're like a deer caught in the headlights, it's super useful to notice we're in the grip of our conditioned tendency, take a breath, ground and centre the body, and have other options available. For the most part fight, flight, freeze and fold are less than resourceful states. Instead how about discernment, eloquence, choice, declining, accepting, knowing what we want and being able to get our needs met?

Life offers us daily opportunities to practice grounding under pressure, some run of the mill and others more dramatic.

I may have chosen a frothy frock for my wedding, but many of the other traditions didn't interest me, particularly the one about being late. I'm rarely late. It makes me anxious and I could only imagine the impact on Paul (although it has to be said, if anyone could tolerate lateness in another, it's my enduringly patient husband). So I set off for the church with my matron of honour in an appropriately vintage car, from the 1940s or thereabouts, with plenty of time. About halfway there, excited and joyous, I looked around and realised, with increasing horror that I'd forgotten the bouquets. We both had. Granted, I don't usually have to check for bouquets when I leave the house, this being the first and hopefully only time in my life when I'll be required to do so. Clearly we had to turn back. What bride could walk down the aisle without her bouquet? This involved a tricky manoeuvre in a narrow country lane and navigating a shallow ford. Worrying given the age of the automobile. Now I *was* anxious. Rushing into the hotel, picking up my skirts and pelting up the stairs to rescue the bouquets, I became seriously distressed. Back in the car Kimberly and I looked at each other and, with a smile, recited the thoroughly familiar serenity prayer in unison:

'God, grant me the serenity to accept the things I cannot change, the courage the change the things I can and the wisdom to know the difference.'

There was nothing to do but keep smiling, keep breathing, ground and centre myself and trust he'd wait. He did. And the video proves we beamed like a couple of teenagers throughout the proceedings. All was well.

In stark contrast, visiting my dementia-ridden mother in the care home was a truly dreadful experience. She didn't know me. Her increasing frailty, diminishing capacity to even hold up her head or engage with the world at any level was harrowing to witness. How the nursing staff endured in such an environment I'll never know. There came the day when they let us know she was fading fast. I planned my usual brief visit, more to assuage my guilt than anything else, when a nurse stopped me in my tracks and gently suggested I might want to say goodbye to her. I was shocked. What a concept. What a seriously good idea yet I had no idea how to attempt such a thing. So I did what I knew to do and took a deep breath, spent time outside in nature and went back inside the dim, depressing room. I grounded and centred myself as if my life depended on it. Certainly my conscience depended on it. And I managed my farewells.

Dramatic examples like these illustrate pivotal moments. The mundane are less striking yet perhaps more important, for they make up the day-to-day existence shaping us time and again. When someone offers me something I don't want – one of those free sachets of a mega-face cream – will I cave in to the pressure, or decline with ease? When the drinks order gets mixed up and suddenly I have the taste of unwanted alcohol in my mouth, will I keep drinking or send it back? When sweet treats assigned for visitors sing to me from the kitchen cupboard, will I be tempted by their dulcet tones, or keep resisting? If I can ground and centre in the face of these smaller tasks, I'm more likely able to manage the big ones. For what we know is *practise makes permanent.* (You may be familiar with 'practise makes perfect' … yet I prefer the other one, believing perfection isn't something to aim for at all, it's impossible.) Here's both the good news and the bad news: what we repeat we get really good at. Research[8] suggests it takes three hundred repetitions to get something into muscle memory and three thousand repetitions to effect embodied change – if we want to either establish something new or change something which has been embodied over time, it will take three thousand repetitions for the new process to be automatic, unconscious. For example, suppose we wanted to shift from right-hand dominant to left-hand dominant, it's going to take that long. And for mastery[9] research suggests ten thousand repetitions.

Practise makes Permanent

Practise makes permanent is both the good news and the bad news here. For we are practising something all of the time, whether we know it or not. There are the things we deliberately practise – the violin or piano, tennis, golf, rowing, learning to read and spell, cooking, typing, sewing,

DIY, photography, driving – and then there are the things out of our awareness. Breathing, chewing, observing, humming, walking, sitting and standing. Aside from the natural human impulses there are a whole host of things we have to learn from scratch. Remember tying your shoelaces for the first time? Brushing your teeth? Riding a bike? Cooking? What we practise we get really good at.

This goes for the things we want to master as well as the things we'd rather not. I learned to type forty years ago. I don't need to look at the keys, can maintain a conversation simultaneously, and type like the wind. A tremendous asset in this keyboard driven era, I'm grateful for the skill. But I don't remember thinking how useful it would be to worry. And I'm really good at worrying. I worry about what time it is, if I'm going to be late, if someone else is going to be late, if I'm dressed appropriately for the occasion, if my heel will break, if I have enough cash, if I'll get lost, if the car will break down, if the train will crash, if Paul will get home safely, that someone I know will die today… you get the idea. Actually, I'm exaggerating only slightly. Such thoughts meander through my mind most days. They used to be at seventy to eighty percent volume, now they're at five to ten percent. Big relief. And when I'm stressed about something – like going to the dentist, getting on a plane, running a workshop – the volume increases slightly. I've developed all kinds of techniques to manage these intrusive thoughts over the years, and the most useful has been dropping into the body, breathing, feeling the ground underneath my feet and looking to the sky to get some perspective.

What else do I practise? I admit, a variety of useful and less useful things. Perhaps most importantly I practise staying sober every single day. I take care of my mental and emotional health as best I can, engaging in meditation, self-care and self-compassion, creative and spiritual pursuits, exercise, learning, being in the natural landscape, exploring new things and maintaining important relationships. And I also do things that don't serve me – I catch myself worrying or getting stressed, eating for solace rather than hunger, watching trash TV, wasting time without the benefit of being relaxed, wandering to social media without need, isolating or withdrawing. That's why I don't use the word 'perfect'. Perfect is an impossible goal. Realising that helps me to accept my fallible, flawed human self, deeply imperfect yet fabulous in that imperfection. And knowing practise makes permanent helps to remind me to move towards the things that serve and increasingly away from the things that don't.

Being a Psychotherapist

The Clare welcoming Bill into her therapy practice in 1999 didn't know all this yet. She was eleven years sober, excited to be in her first year of training at Strozzi

Institute, regularly commuting the four-hour drive to Petaluma. In some ways we were both on the brink of powerful change. I was beginning the next chapter of my personal and professional development with Strozzi; Bill was committing to sustained and quality sobriety. Perhaps both being in this vulnerable state of flux made a difference? I believe our mutual courage influenced the work – deepening it – allowing both subtle and significant change to unfold. Perhaps breaking down my own barriers in Strozzi's somatic work enabled Bill to do the same. Undoubtedly my emerging confidence and embodiment as a sober practitioner contributed massively to what we could produce together.

I'm reminded of Marianne Williamson's beautiful quote from *A Return to Love: Reflections on the Principles of a Course in Miracles*:

> Our deepest fear is not that we are in-adequate. Our deepest fear is that we are powerful beyond measure. It is our light, not our darkness that most frightens us. We ask ourselves, Who am I to be brilliant, gorgeous, talented, fabulous? Actually, who are you not to be? You are a child of God. Your playing small does not serve the world. There is nothing enlightened about shrinking so that other people won't

feel insecure around you. We are all meant to shine, as children do. We were born to make manifest the glory of God that is within us. It is not just in some of us; it is in everyone. And as we let our own light shine, we unconsciously give other people permission to do the same. As we are liberated from our own fear, our presence automatically liberates others.

I strongly believe practitioners can only take their clients where they have been themselves. If I'm scared of my own anger, how can I facilitate a client getting in touch with and processing theirs? If I'm overly contained (tight and held, impeding impulses to be in movement or expression) then I'm likely to pass on both that skill and an unconscious expectation for others to be equally contained. I wax lyrical about the work at Strozzi Institute because without a somatic approach to my own development I wouldn't have been able to facilitate transformation for so many clients over the last decade. As I let my own light shine, so Bill was given permission to embrace his inherent goodness.

CHAPTER THREE

Working with Bill

Being a Veteran

> *At an age when most young men are typically forming lasting ideas about life and intimacy (Erickson, 1968), soldiers in Vietnam were losing friends in violent ways, and perhaps learning that closeness hurts too much.*[10]

Bill's life changed forever the day he received the draft for Vietnam on 7 January 1967. He was just nineteen, and a young nineteen at that.

We dwelled neither on *how* he got there nor on what happened *when* he got there – it was too painful – but we did explore the impact of those experiences. To say his life had been devastated would not be an exaggeration. He may have eventually pulled himself up by his bootstraps and through years of hard work established a business that now employed a dozen men who were like family to him. But he'd never married, never had the children he'd dreamed of – he'd been unable to sustain a relationship. I felt such sadness and compassion for this kind, gentle man who deserved so much.

Bill provided my first opportunity to work with a Vietnam veteran. Looking back I can say I was less than well-equipped. I knew about trauma and alcoholism, but all I knew about the Vietnam War was what I'd been exposed to on TV and in the movies (Oliver Stone's 1989 movie *Born on the Fourth of July* and Adrian Lyne's 1998 movie *Jacob's Ladder*). The war began before I was born, escalated during my childhood in the UK and officially came to a close when I was eighteen – I simply hadn't been exposed to the relentless media coverage prevailing in the US.

The extent to which Bill didn't want to talk about Vietnam reflected both my own discomfort and strong belief that, in some cases – this being one – reporting the *detail* of the trauma is not necessary to *resolve* the trauma. He remembered little of his first tour in 1967, although knew it to be a 'bad' year, recalling more of the second tour that followed. No details though; Bill shared nothing of the day-to-day experience there. I reflected on his opening words to me, that he had some 'tough things' to talk about, and I wondered if he was protecting me from the horror? If that was so, then I hold up my hand and acknowledge I willingly colluded with him. Morrie, his first civilian therapist, told me he did the same. Perhaps he debriefed at the Veterans Administration's treatment centre where he was admitted for twenty-one days sometime after his return home for alcoholism treatment? I doubt it though – it was customary for Vets to be demobbed directly onto commercial jets, alone and still in mud-splattered camouflage. My hopes for any useful debriefing were not high.[11]

Unusually, Bill hadn't experimented with alcohol while growing up, partly in response to seeing his father drunk, and partly because he much preferred to be out in nature, exploring the rich landscape of Hawaii in his free time. He only began to drink when drafted, initially to engender a sense of belonging with his comrades-in-arms, later to numb the psychological and emotional pain. He was not alone.[12]

Bill was a gentle soul, and a complicated one. His relationships to both alcohol and aggression were multi-faceted. On one hand he identified as a coward; on the other, he could explode into uncontrollable rage – both sides of this coin scared him. He told me of a time at a football game in school when someone called him a 'stupid *haole*' and this time, rather than run away, Bill reported he beat the offender up 'pretty good' to the extent his principal commented, 'You could have disfigured that kid.' These complexities kept him company better than any friend. Yet the same complexities were as devastating as the enemy.

As I look back now, researching what Bill's Vietnam experience may have encompassed, I'm embarrassed to have known so little. All I know is that he was a radio operator, required to carry a full pack and heavy radio as well, being regularly targeted to disrupt communication. I learned the life expectancy of a radio operator in a firefight was fifteen seconds. A commentator at the time said: That big antenna sticking high in the air was a dead giveaway, like a big arrow pointing downward saying, "Here I am, shoot me!"[13] I think how lucky he was to have survived, and along with the hundreds of thousands of others, how great the cost. They came home, not to a welcome, but to judgment and ostracism, often spat at in the streets.

Creating Safety and Stability – Getting Started

With every client the work begins by building trust. Without a safe, holding container in the treatment room for Bill to step into, anything else simply wouldn't work. He needed to know I would be on time, maintain boundaries, fulfil on promises, share my expertise, maintain confidentiality, tell the truth, be fair and firm, honour my word, listen attentively and be fully present. A tall order. And less about being perfect and more about being consistent, apologising when I wasn't, acknowledging the human fallibility I brought to our time together as a way to meet his frailties, meeting his vulnerabilities.

At the outset we agreed that abstinence was paramount. Bill identified with Brendan Behan's famous quote: 'One drink is too many for me and a thousand not enough.' Where drinking used to be an organising principle, Bill had already found successful ways to abstain for long periods – these practices would be maintained and hopefully enhanced with the embodied approach to recovery that was my forté.

Influenced by my somatic training with Strozzi Institute we began by designing a declaration to guide Bill in his every thought and decision:

> For the sake of maintaining my sobriety,
> peace and serenity
>
> I am a stand for faith, I am a commitment
> to courage, and I belong here

Bill chose each word carefully, meaningful to him beyond the dictionary definition, and this became a powerful source of inspiration. Committed to memory, he used it like a mantra, a reminder of his substance, his identity, his power. In stark contrast to the bullied youngster at school, he blossomed in the face of having his very own personal brand. He strongly desired not only sobriety but also peace and serenity, absent for much of his life. His faith in a Higher Power – God most days – was key, and having felt such shame about being a coward, mention of the word courage was crucial. I felt touched by his reference to belonging, referencing both the true sense of the word and also his desire for living life to the fullest.

Memorising a declaration is not enough. It needs the support of daily actions and practices – building new habits. I explain this by comparing it to the construction of a new building. First draw the design, the outcome desired; then put the foundations in place; next, support the emerging structure with scaffolding; finally make it watertight with a roof. If Bill's declaration provided the foundation on which to stand, now we needed to build the containing walls and supporting scaffolding simultaneously, no easy task.

Creating Safety and Stability – Moving Ahead with Practices

Practices provide the container in which we can tolerate change. Change is a funny thing. Everything changes all the time – weather, mood, growth, decay – yet the very things we want to change personally seem the most difficult to shift, even when we put our attention there. When we do something over and over again, it becomes automatic. We don't have to think about the components of the action, they simply flow together. So replacing those unconscious activities requires this kind of process: notice the action, pause to acknowledge we're doing something familiar, stopping, then replacing with something else which feels both uncomfortable and counter-intuitive. Definitely not easy.

New practices are particularly tricky because we have a tendency to do things we're good at, preferring to avoid looking clumsy as beginners inevitably do. Ever tried juggling? (For those who have, pick something else!) The coordination involved in handling multiple balls at once – the rhythm of throwing and catching, assessing the space involved – all rather awkward manoeuvres. Watching someone juggling seamlessly belies the underlying practise it's taken to get there.[14]

Grounding is one of the first things I learned in my somatic training, its origins in the martial arts. It involves dropping the attention down into the body from the head, where most of us reside most of the time, paying attention to our connection to the earth and the interior landscape of the body we inhabit. Grounding provides the basis for becoming present in-this-very-moment. It's the quality I found so compelling about my first sight of Dr Richard Strozzi-Heckler.

For those in recovery, having the skill to check in with the body is essential. Exposed to alcohol at every turn (adverts, shops, liquor stores, pubs, bars, restaurants, etc.), the recovering alcoholic needs to recognise sensation in the body to assess how they feel in the face of alcohol and its temptation. 'Am I safe to go somewhere where alcohol is available? Would it be better to avoid the place altogether? Could I have someone go with me?' If paid attention to, sensations inform the level of desire and susceptibility. In Bill's case, he reported times when he could be around alcohol and have zero motivation to drink, yet other times when he didn't remember making the choice to drink – he'd simply wind up passed out several days later and not know how he got there. So he needed to pay attention to his internal sensations so that they would become his ally.

Having paid little attention to his body before, other than as a means to carry around his head, or as the recipient of painful medical procedures, teaching Bill to ground and centre proved challenging. I shared an appropriately limited version of the dog-on-the-beach-story to demonstrate the importance of learning this new skill. We persevered. I don't believe we were entirely successful. However, there was a peripheral benefit. Bill did begin to pay more attention to his breath and reported an increased ability to manage anxiety at meetings, giving presentations, in difficult conversations, and in the maelstrom of life when he'd prefer to be alone.

Thought stopping is part of a suite of classic practices I learned at The Matrix Institute on Addictions in the early 1990s. Basically a cognitive-behavioural technique, the idea is to notice an alcohol-related thought and replace it with some kind of STOP sign (or foot on the brake, or switch off a light). I recommend adding in two more things: declaring the word 'stop' out aloud, and moving. If sitting, stand; if standing, sit or wriggle. It doesn't have to be a big movement (although that may really help) but shifting the physiology embeds the experience in an embodied manner. We want to teach the body something very different about alcohol. No longer a *start*, but a *stop*. No longer a *go*, but a *halt*.

Despite my best efforts, Bill wasn't terribly impressed with thought stopping. We tried lots of alternatives in the hope of finding something to capture his imagination. Even having post-it notes with a STOP sign in his truck, where he spent a huge amount of time, and around his home and office didn't assist. What he *could* do with ease was take a breath. He could recognise the thought, stop what he was doing, take a breath and be gentle with himself. Sometimes.

Trigger awareness goes hand in hand with thought stopping. Given the barrage of direct, let alone indirect, alcohol triggers in the daily environment, knowing those triggers supports their management. Some can be avoided, some cannot. Those common to him and many others include: seeing alcohol in adverts (billboards, TV, magazines, sponsorship) or seeing people drink alcohol (same again plus in bars, restaurants, homes, occasionally on the street, during leisure activities such as sailing, bowling, fishing, barbecuing); physical presence of alcohol (when grocery shopping, in people's homes, bars, restaurants). Add in hearing about or smelling alcohol in these settings as well. For these reasons, it is important to maintain an alcohol-free zone at home, to which Bill was committed. Aside from obvious bottles of liquor, we reviewed possibilities for hidden alcohol in the home: mouthwash, vanilla extract, some vinegars, over-the-counter cough and cold remedies, and some homeopathic remedies.

We started with alcohol in all its forms, moving on to the complicated terrain of feelings, emotions, behaviours – taking many hours identifying, exploring and planning for their presence. We addressed Bill's feelings of loneliness and abandonment, anxiety, depression, sadness, fear, pain, shame, disappointment, failure. Even relaxation was complex – sometimes it helped, other times it lowered his inhibitions and he drank.

I often wondered how an hour a week could possibly address the layers and complexity he faced on a daily basis. AA suggests 'keep it simple' and uses an acronym for triggers – HALT (Hungry Angry Lonely Tired) – a good place to start but woefully inadequate. In addition there was a web of interconnected feelings and emotions, commonly experienced not just in the worst of times, but in mediocrity as well.

Rather than design a specific response to each trigger described, being too intertwined to separate out, we designed an overall plan of attack for Bill's frequently triggered state. As anyone familiar with mindfulness and presence already knows, being able to track sensation and experience moment to moment is the most useful resource in this endeavour. Within this the key skills of grounding and centring were neither attractive nor easy for Bill, so we focused on his ability to pay attention to the breath, thereby slowing things down. Similar to thought stopping, the process of pause-breathe-respond moved his body more towards rest-digest and away from fight-flight, helping him to slow his pulse, heart-rate and reactivity. In all honesty, sometimes this worked well and sometimes it didn't. I suspect I didn't build enough relevance for him to commit to mindfulness, or it was too hard, or he didn't practise enough when he didn't need the resource, or all of the above.

Having reviewed the plethora of predictable and unpredictable triggers, we moved on to consider the huge variety of recovery-oriented activities which weren't triggering. Some really positive things appeared on this list: waking up, listening to upbeat or classical music, walking in nature, being with his cats, driving around for work, listening to inspirational tapes and CDs, chewing gum, eating well, going to the beach, resting, reading sci-fi, meditation and prayer.

Recovery-oriented practices include paying attention to health. For Bill, this was an essential element given his recovery from cancer and alcoholism. He needed no convincing of the benefits of exercise, healthy food choices and enough water, although like many, putting them into practice was another matter.

Bill's depression, managed with a combination of anti-depressant medication and life-style choices, required constant monitoring. I recommended a mood and depression chart, one that he could complete morning and night with a simple number out of ten – the goal was consistent zero to three, low-level warning for four or five, medium-level warning for six, and high-level warning for seven or above. He designed his own chart, for this actually really appealed to his methodical engineering temperament. He preferred to use colours, with pale yellow for zero to three, yellow for four or five, orange for six, and red for seven or above. Just glancing at the bar chart gave us both a sense of where he was. Of course, it worked well when he was in pale yellow territory, occasionally alerted him appropriately in yellow, and by the time he was in orange, he tended not to have the responsive capacity we'd pre-planned. This could range from calling a recovering friend, to being more active in his recovery groups and speaking up about how he felt, to calling me or calling his psychiatrist. I think the theory here was sound; perhaps the execution left something to be desired, but it was better than no monitoring at all.

Another facet of his health involved attending medical and dental appointments. As could be anticipated, he loathed them both, especially the dentist. Being no stranger to dental fear myself, I recommended a course of hypnotherapy with a colleague, and this really helped him manage his fears about dental procedures. As to the doctor and cancer specialists, he was by then attending for routine annual checks and we made sure to schedule our meetings immediately before and after for any support needed.

For many, recovery-oriented practices involve attendance at twelve-step meetings, and AA was a great choice in theory. However, Bill's shyness, introversion and sensitivity weren't conducive to engaging with the recovery community, at least in those first months. As developing a support system is key, twelve-step or otherwise, if there was failure anywhere in Bill's treatment experience with me, then it was there.

Developing a support system is an essential element for those in recovery. Indeed, as Johann Hari claims in his thought-provoking book *Chasing the Scream*, 'The opposite of addiction is not sobriety, the opposite of addiction is connection.' While I'm inclined to disagree and claim instead, 'The opposite of addiction is sobriety WITH connection,' I take his point.

Many people benefit tremendously from the support system the twelve-step community provides. And many do not. Rather than an esoteric debate about the good and the bad, the rights and wrongs, I'm interested in exploring what didn't work for Bill, and in retrospect, what may have worked more effectively. I believe it was Bill's lack of all-around support system that let him down the most.

Those family members still alive were at a distance, both geographically and emotionally, so of little help. He was not the kind of man to pick up the phone either to chat or ask for help. His Vietnam comrades were equally out of reach – either killed in action, impaired themselves, or unavailable because Bill chose to keep them at arm's length. Reminders of that time were simply too painful to bear. Even men and women he'd been to residential treatment with after Vietnam were long lost. Any friends he'd made since were more like acquaintances than close buddies. Women he'd had fleeting relationships with were not appropriate for this type of support; equally his employees were off-limits for similar reasons. Consequently, he was left pretty high and dry. Perhaps most importantly, Bill's ability to connect, his capacity to engage in friendship, was significantly impaired.

We're back to shame – trauma – addiction and the resultant toll.

Bill was unable to trust those he most needed to in life – his parents. Dad was a functioning alcoholic, emotionally unavailable at best, emotionally explosive at worst. Mum was a strict disciplinarian, not exactly the warm fuzzy type nurturing her children to create secure attachment. Let me be clear, I'm not blaming them, for it's likely they were simply replicating the parenting they had themselves, simply stating facts. So he learned early on that people weren't trustworthy, and even though he craved deep connection more than anything, he hadn't developed the capacity to recognise or exploit it in others. (With the possible exception of his employees, and that's another story because he didn't have to be intimate with them.) In fact, if someone showed up who was trust-worthy, Bill would likely run a mile in the other direction for fear of the overwhelming nature of the intimacy possible.

Add to this mix the sense of shame Bill carried around with him 24/7, believing that he was fundamentally flawed, and we find someone unable to 'fix' the flaw, drawn to equally flawed others who he attempted to caretake or fix instead. His fleeting relationships with women along the way reflected the strong pull to rescue – he was drawn to those in abusive relationships needing a way out, other alcoholics or addicts active in their substance abuse, untreated women sexually or physically abused as children, those with other mental health problems such as depression or anxiety, even one who sounded to me – from his description – as someone with dissociative identity disorder (previously called multiple personality disorder).

It would seem that a ready-made, well-established support system like AA would be ideal. Well, yes and no. Whatever else AA provides, it offers consistent, predictable support, often with the same faces at meetings over and over again. It offers the possibility of a sponsor, someone who volunteers their time to mentor those new to the programme, a dedicated 'best friend' if you will. It offers a core structure, easy to follow and read about in books and literature. It offers a network of ready-made 'friends' who routinely offer time and phone numbers to those in need. It unofficially offers what's called 'the meeting after the meeting' wherein members go for coffee after the formal meeting is complete, an opportunity to cross-talk and chat in an easy-going environment. Ideal. Yes, it offers all of this, assuming someone has the capacity to connect, chat, be vulnerable, engage, communicate, ask for help and support, say yes and no with confidence, draw boundaries. Do you see the challenge with this? Bill could navigate the professional waters of his business life well enough; navigating the personal waters of intimacy was another matter. Apart from shame and trauma informing every breath, he was shy and introvert to boot. AA on paper was an excellent fit for him; in practice, not so much.

Of course, AA was not the only game in town. There were other ready-made support systems: SMART Recovery,[15] SOS (Secular Organisation for Sobriety),[16] and the Christian organisation Celebrate Recovery.[17] Men for Sobriety (an offshoot of Women for Sobriety)[18] and LifeRing Secular Recovery[19] were not available at that time. Even though there were fewer meeting options, that really wasn't the point. Any organised gathering of people, no matter their affiliation, was going to be triggering for Bill. We ground to a halt. He didn't want to join a church even though his religious beliefs didn't get in the way of him doing so. Every other community organisation we looked at – Rotary, Freemasonry, The Buffs, Loyal Order of Moose, etc. – had alcohol consumption as part of their social structure, so all were discounted and in any event, we were squarely confronting the central issue of connection and intimacy. It was even more important, therefore, for Bill to develop some new skills.

We began with two of the essentials. Firstly, self-soothing to decrease anxiety. Secondly, in preparation for connecting with others, we worked on Bill practising how to ask for support, how to set boundaries and how to boldly say yes or no.

Self-soothing is a fundamental skill for people in recovery. At its simplest, alcohol is about self-medicating distress, whether it be generated by external or internal stimuli. Alcohol becomes the soothing balm to dissolve discomfort, just as pain-killers manage toothache. We looked for means of self-soothing that Bill could access alone on the road, in public places, at work – in short, whether alone or with people. For some, grounding and centring, paying attention to the breath, relaxing down into the body, feels soothing. Sadly, this didn't work well for Bill. Slowing down his breathing helped calm anxiety, but couldn't be described as soothing. Petting his cats was soothing, so we had a resource for when at home, and this clued me in to what may be useful elsewhere – something kinaesthetic involving touch and stroking. Not yet trained myself, we turned to a hypnotherapy/ neurolinguistic programming (NLP) practitioner colleague for assistance, who taught Bill a number of useful techniques. These included deep relaxation to assist getting to sleep at night, something we called 'attention training' rather than meditation (too 'out there' for Bill's taste), accessing a relaxed and resourced state he could fire off with an anchor (rubbing his outer thigh, so something he could do in most scenarios).

When Bill remembered to use the self-soothing strategies, they worked well. The challenge is that he forgot. Or remembered too late. Or felt embarrassed in public in case someone would think him weird. Or his inner self-critical dialogue would get the better of him, shaming and judging, and he'd spiral towards bleakness. Nevertheless, we kept focusing on when the strategies worked, congratulating him respectfully, and gradually building his confidence and self-esteem.

In preparation for connecting with others, I mentioned several building blocks: asking for help and support, setting boundaries, saying yes and no with clarity, building capacity for intimacy. All these activities required Bill to tolerate anxious sensations, so we utilised Strozzi Institute's *partner practices*, described in detail in Dr Richard Strozzi-Heckler's book *The Anatomy of Change*.

For example, learning to say no and set boundaries would look like this: After explaining in detail what we were about to experiment with, demonstrating myself first, and getting his agreement to proceed, Bill and I stood on opposite sides of the office, about four metres/yards apart. We faced one another. On occasions when this was too triggering for him – evidenced by an automatic appeasing smile, shallow breathing, a slight flush through the skin visible in his upper torso – I would step slightly to the left or right so we weren't exactly eye to eye albeit still four metres/yards away. I led us through a spoken grounding and centring process, checking in with Bill about what he noticed. If he felt secure, stable and safe enough to proceed, we did so.

When ready for me to approach, Bill would signal in some way that kept him grounded, and I would begin walking towards him gently and very slowly, yet with clear intention to connect. The moment he began to feel even a hint of discomfort or distress, his job was to signal me to halt. This could be with an audible 'no' or 'stop', raising his hand palm facing me, taking a step himself, or any other means in the moment which made sense. I paid careful attention to responding to his gesture, a key piece of this trust-building exercise. Initially, Bill would react with an automatic appeasing smile, his head inclining very slightly to one side and towards me. He had difficulty saying anything audible or making a motion with his arm. We kept practising until he gained enough confidence and comfort to do so. Early on I could take four or five steps towards him before he gesticulated and as time went by he played with saying 'no' very soon after I'd moved. He was surprised how difficult this turned out to be. After all, he was a successful businessman with a team of people working for him, yet, in this environment, where much was at stake and there was the possibility for real connection, he had a much different experience. He warmed to the process, and we utilised partner practices like these regularly.

Sober at Last

Seven months after we began working together, on 25 July 2000, Bill celebrated three years of sobriety.

The longest he'd ever been continually sober, this was a significant achievement. He had a few sober friends now; he was taking good care of his health – eating regularly, remembering to drink water throughout the day. He even exercised in the morning on awakening. He ensured some down time at the weekend, either on his boat or at home with his beloved cats. I felt hopeful for the future; so did he.

Less than forty days later he went on a bender and needed three days detox in hospital. He admitted he was very scared. The medication Librium[20] helped, yet its mood and mind-altering powers took him 'to scary places'. He didn't elaborate but research suggests[21] it can cause hallucinations and I wondered if any PTSD-related Vietnam experiences had occurred. Shame had certainly flared. He looked utterly wretched. Eyes downcast, mumbling in his beard, evasive in his answers and on the verge of tears, it was a delicate time. I decided he needed compassionate attention followed by a definitive plan of action to keep him sober. Abstinence remained the goal. Moderation wasn't within his capability and certainly wouldn't serve him.

I'm sad to report Bill's relapses continued. Even though we know relapse is a component of alcoholism, we – practitioners and clients alike – always hope for enduring recovery. I became the more grateful for my own unin-terrupted recovery and wanted this for him as well. He'd suffered so much already! The rescuer in me desperately wanted him to be rewarded for all he'd gone through – being a *haole*, Vietnam, childless, partner-less, cancer – and yet his own belief system suggested otherwise. I was aghast to hear him say, 'The part of me that's connected with God knows what's right and wrong. He designed for this to be hard as a punishment.'

Nevertheless, we continued to meet regularly to review his sober plan and how he fared. The next relapse could, perhaps, have been predicted.

Pressure began to build in November 2000, when extensive media coverage was given to President Bill Clinton's visit to Vietnam, the first US President to visit since the end of the Vietnam War. I watched him as his memories were evoked and he began to withdraw into his protective shell. He couldn't bring himself to accept a sober pal's invitation to Thanksgiving dinner, staying home alone. I felt concerned about his darkening mood and we worked out a disciplined routine that involved consciously avoiding what we called 'Liquor Alley' at the grocery store, and specifically when stocking up with provisions for his Christmas trip. We also set up meetings over the entire holiday period, augmented by other sober support – he missed them all.

Emerging from the Confusion

When Bill eventually showed up mid-January 2001 he looked terrible. Depressed, dejected, tired, haggard, clothes looser around his middle, hair unkempt and beard shaggier than usual, my worst fears were realised. This was how Bill looked post-binge. He came in eyes and head downcast, mumbling apologies, filled with shame and self-loathing. Stumbling and tearful, he told his story.

On Christmas Day, alone and on the boat, thoughts turned to receiving the draft on 7 January thirty-four years ago, and his mood became bleak. He focused on all the losses – no partner, no children, parents both gone now, Vietnam buddies, other friends as well – a sense of complete hopelessness overtook him, an overwhelming desire to numb it all out took charge. He pulled in to port sometime between Christmas and New Year and stocked up. Enough for a week-long binge. He didn't remember getting home and had some sense – simply based on the calendar – that he'd been lying in a darkened room, feeling sick, filled with self-loathing, attempting to manage the DT's which inevitably took hold. These are not times when alcoholics like Bill can reach out for help, to me or anyone else.

Under normal circumstances I wouldn't consider bodywork with a client so soon after a binge but he was desperate and just wanted the pain to end. He returned later that week for a somatic bodywork session, described in full in the *Prologue*. Amongst Bill's many bodywork sessions, it remains the most transformative and significant, although it didn't propel him to sustained sobriety.

Stormy Waters

We continued sessions through that spring, meeting once or twice a week, the second session of the week devoted to somatic bodywork. I want to report something miraculous, but the truth is Bill remained in stormy waters. Some months he maintained a couple of weeks sobriety, some months it was a roundabout of a few days sober and a few days drinking. While I truly believe the bodywork was finally helping him to release traumatic toxicity stored for decades, I also believe he had insufficient support to endure what was being stirred without resorting to his best friend for solace. May, June and July remained unsettled and I fiercely expressed my concern. Bill finally agreed to attend an out-patient treatment facility, unwilling to give up the helm of his business for an in-patient stay.

I'm grateful he had the support of an established sober support group by the time of the 9/11 attack on the World Trade Centre in New York. It was a similar moment to hearing about John F. Kennedy's assassination, or Princess Diana's death: I will always remember where I was and what I was doing at that time. Seeing the plane fly into the second tower on TV that fateful morning shook me to my core. I was in Palo Alto, California, about to see clients that day. Everyone cancelled. The terrorist attack happened three thousand miles away, yet the whole country was in mourning. Our sense of safety violated, we all sought to make sense of something so inexplicable.

I wondered how Bill would be; I knew it wouldn't be good. Depressed and tormented? His words at our next session haunted me: 'Those people died in dread. I know what that's like. It was all around, no escape.' Clearly, he was reflecting on Vietnam. He continued, explaining that images of the *squads* [22] were loud and persistent. 'I just fixed radios,' he said, shrugging his shoulders. Then he seemed to drift away, retreating into another world, inaccessible to me, and as a cloud passed over his face I heard him say under his breath, 'Some will die.' This was the most he'd ever said about Vietnam. So little, yet so much.

At a loss, all I could do was be present for him. There were no words to soothe, nothing would offer solace in the darkness. We sat in companionable silence, occasionally making fleeting eye contact, mostly separated by a wall of anguish.

The weeks and months rolled by. His commitment to

out-patient treatment served him well and he maintained sobriety. The plan we designed a year ago seemed to take hold. My concerns about the triggering impact of the war now raging in Afghanistan were unfounded. This was a just war in Bill's mind; troops returned to a hero's welcome and much greater support from the VA than he'd received. He was able to make sense of the news reports, feel a kinship, albeit at arm's length; a sense of redemption. I kept my own feelings appropriately under wraps. The focus remained on Bill and his sobriety.

The more stable he became, the more his thoughts turned to the future and a deep desire to take care of the men and women who worked for him. While his cancer was in remission, he was under no illusion about his longevity and wanted to 'make things right'. I think he was beginning to come to terms with not having children, the unlikelihood at this stage, and his loyal employees would be officially recognised instead. I reflected on the redemption at work here too. He may not have been able to save his comrades-in-arms, nor be a father, yet here he could make a resounding contribution to people who cared for him, remaining loyal through some of his darkest days. He began to meet attorneys and get things in order. I had the utmost admiration for his determination.

Paying attention to his own future, Bill's courageous responsibility triggered something in me. *Our synergy worked both ways.* The space wasn't solely created by me, it was the natural product of the way we met one another – consistently stepping in to mutual trust, respect, love and care. When I was appropriately vulnerable, that gave permission to Bill to acknowledge and attend to his own; when he was bold, there was an infectious quality. It was as if we stepped in to a boat together, sometimes his hand on the tiller, sometimes mine, allowing the downstream flow to maintain momentum. We became more than the sum of our parts.

So at the turn of the century, in my forties and dissatisfied with life – particularly on the relationship front – I confronted my fears and began exploring options.

People are Waiting

A colleague introduced me to a remarkable woman called Dorthy Tyo. Founder of the Palo Alto School of Hypnotherapy and an instructor there, Dorthy is also a Medical Hypnotherapist and Medical Intuitive. She has the kind of warm presence which envelopes you in blanket of velvety softness yet, make no mistake, she's also a keen businesswoman. Drawn to her wisdom and skill, I arranged a session to explore my dissatisfaction.

Three noteworthy things came out of that meeting: an angel card I still carry in my wallet; an ability to charge full fee without flinching; and a decision to move from my beloved San Luis Obispo to Palo Alto. Perhaps this sounds far-fetched, yet something unfolded in the course of our time together that was momentous. Dorthy's ability to hold the space, see what I couldn't see (both in the worldly and non-worldly planes), say things which revealed opportunities heretofore unavailable comes from – I believe – innate gifts, talents and an enormous amount of experience. I certainly aspire to achieve such empathic presence and attunement in my sessions with clients.

At the beginning of our meeting I picked an angel card, not to be opened until the end. Then we explored my life, unpacking the highlights of my history, my deep desire for a partner, and what kept getting in the way. She was gentle and kind, yet firm and direct. I shared the ambivalence I felt about remaining in SLO, a place I loved yet somehow knew wasn't going to offer up a life-partner. It was then she said: 'There are people waiting for you.' She took my breath away. At first I thought she meant my man was waiting in Palo Alto, then when she repeated, 'There are *people* here waiting for you,' I realised that was not her meaning. She was talking about clients waiting for me. Still, we hear what we want to hear, and I left convinced the love of my life *and* clients awaited.

In a bit of a daze – for this changed everything – I got out my cheque book and asked how much, actually having no idea. I remember her saying 'one hundred and seventy-five dollars' which was a substantial sum in those days (we're talking 2002). I wrote the numbers with ease. Actually, if she'd said 'five hundred dollars' I would have done the same. What had been imparted was priceless. For in that moment I truly understood for the first time that they were *just numbers*. Numbers representing an energetic exchange. Perhaps it would take me two client sessions to pay for this one, for others it would have taken a day's work, yet money comes and money goes in a kind of energetic dance all around us. From that time forward I had no difficulty asking for some figure representing my worth. Dorthy was an exemplar of self-worth and self-value, and I learned a great lesson.

And there's more. At the end of the session was also the angel card to consult:

> We must be wiling to relinquish the life we've planned, so as to have the life that is waiting for us.
> – *Joseph Campbell*

I was gobsmacked. I'd picked this from amongst many at the outset, not as a result of her defining words. Synchronicity, or what? Whether serendipity or chance, I left our session with excitement and trepidation. Yes! I was going to move to the Bay Area, how extraordinary.

And oh sh*t, this meant I had to close my practice in SLO. What would this mean for Bill?

Anguish

I'm no stranger to moving. From the UK to Dallas, on to Nashville and then Philadelphia, finally settling in and around California for almost two decades. But this move felt different. This was the first time I had a thriving private practice to close, and in my worst moments I was awash with fear and shame, worried I was abandoning clients for selfish reasons. My therapist and supervisor supported me through the transition, guiding and encouraging me.

With the benefit of hindsight, I see a bigger picture now. This is truly where I can see the extent to which Bill and I influenced one another, that in the universal scheme of things we were meant to gravitate into one another's orbit.

The mutual respect and love informing our sessions achieved many things: Bill set on the path of recovery, sustaining his sobriety one day at a time, learning self-acceptance and getting his house in order. And for me? I want to say the self-respect he demonstrated allowed me in some way to bolster my own. That he set an example. After all, if a traumatised Vietnam Vet could overcome his sense of shame, learn to love himself, then surely so could I. But there's something else. The healing nature of love, ever present in our interactions, somehow opened me up to an expectation of having someone special in my life. Bill may not have been fortunate enough to find the love of his life, but finally, I became willing to stop kissing frogs and go in search of my prince.

Delivering the News

In all honesty, I have no recollection of telling Bill about leaving. It's all a bit of a fog. I know I was scared. I worried that at worst I was making a selfish decision and in the process abandoning Bill, undoing the good we'd done. But at best, it was time for us *both* to move on.

Bill had been attending out-patient treatment for eight months, had other sober support in the community, including a sponsor, and his reliance on our sessions for stability – as a sober container – was diminishing rather than increasing. He'd learned and implemented so much. He paid attention to his body in a new, healthy manner. He'd never be interested in the benefits of yoga or meditation, but he could now ground himself, feel his feet on the floor, relax his belly and take a deep settling breath to soothe his anxiety.

My notes, sparser than usual, indicate that I told him in March 2002 and we spent the next six months working through all that meant. For him, and privately with my therapist and supervisor, for me.

Something shifts when we have finite time to work rather than a sense of open-endedness. For me there's a confusion of urgency, a desire to pull away prematurely all mixed with an agonising pressure of *not-enough-time-not-enough-space*. Did I have the courage to deepen into conversations which beckoned? Had I done enough of my own emotional / psychological work to endure the excitement of moving and the pain of leaving behind the familiar? Again, few notes exist for this period, so I hope I had the courage.

Referral

Bill's out-patient treatment met his need for sober community support, providing a safer, more contained therapeutic environment than ever a twelve-step meeting could. But it didn't meet his need to be held individually in a therapeutic environment so we talked about who else he might work with after I'd left for the Bay Area. I found this difficult. And I'm embarrassed to acknowledge I found this difficult for surely, if this were purely a therapeutic relationship, it would be easy to simply transfer him to another clinician? But my protective instinct felt like a fierce mother bear wanting to protect her vulnerable cub from harm. That says it all. Would someone else make enough space, take enough care with him?

My supervisor never raised a single eyebrow although

I sometimes anticipated such a response. If I'd been my own supervisor I'm sure I'd have struggled to keep my eyebrows in check. Clearly she was someone I trusted but out of the running for the job herself. So I had to find someone else. I reviewed each of my colleagues for suitability, looking for someone more similar than dissimilar to me. I ruled out the directive, harder-edged, more pedantic practitioners and looked for someone with compassion, their own knowledge of addiction and recovery, someone gentle and reassuring.

I settled on someone called Marie (not her real name, the therapist in question prefers to remain anonymous). Of similar age and experience, we knew each other from the general therapeutic networking circles of the town as well as a sober support group just for therapists. So I knew she walked her talk. Bill agreed to me having a handover conversation with Marie and they subsequently worked together.

Here's what really surprises me. When Morrie and I talked recently (the original referral source), he remembers Bill with clarity and fondness. We reminisced a little, reflecting on our shared care and concern for his wellbeing. Yet when I contacted Marie to get a sense of how she experienced Bill, she had no recollection of him. Zero. I find that astonishing. Perhaps, in the absence of a signed release, she chose to maintain strict ethical boundaries of confidentiality. Perhaps though – and this is certainly my intuitive experience of her response – she simply doesn't remember Bill. What explains the very particular experience we shared as therapist-client, so dissimilar to that with another therapist?

And here I can only rely on instincts. For I know, deep in my bones, that we were meant to influence one another's lives in the way we did. Not in some pre-ordained, fatalistic manner, but as both our lives unfolded there was some serendipitous, synchronistic coming together of mutual benefit. If I'm brave I'll repeat words from the Introduction, that love was present – love perhaps more suitably described as *agape*. If I stay brave I'll also say there was divine intervention. As I believe there was when Bill Wilson and Dr Bob came into one another's lives and ultimately designed the twelve steps of Alcoholics Anonymous[23]. How else could two dysfunctional drunks come up with such a powerful program? One which certainly reflected its time and may benefit from some updates, yet one which endures, decades later, around the globe, for alcohol abuse and much beyond. Bill and I may not have changed the world in the dramatic, global way Bill W. and Dr Bob did, yet in our own small way, we've each made our mark.

Closure

We had our last session on 5 August 2002. Just over two and a half years since that halting phone call in 1999 and much water under the proverbial bridge. I have no recollection of it, no notes, just 'last session'. I can predict we talked about boundaries, about endings, about transferring the baton to Marie. And yet while this may be closure in the clinical sense, I knew it wasn't the end.

CHAPTER FOUR

People Waiting for You

The journey of a thousand miles begins
with one step.
— *Lao Tzu*

A light-bulb moment. The penny drops. Intellectual
insight is accompanied by a felt sense in the body.

These are the moments I cherish in my work. Accompanied by a wash of awareness sweeping across my
client's face, new insight having the clarity of fine crystal,
I am assured we also have the possibility of a fresh
beginning.

Just recently one of these eureka moments got my
attention in a very particular way. It felt profound and
invigorating. Eric and I looked at each other, simply

beaming in the glare of realisation. A piece of information had chosen to reveal itself in this special moment, not before, waiting in the wings for just the right mixture of fertile soil to plant its seed. We both got out of the way and something else emerged in the space.

'Are you saying,' he said as he leaned forward to connect more deeply, 'that because we crave acceptance, connection and belonging, and because I didn't get that as a child, I don't know how to now, even though I'm an adult?'

'Pretty much.' I nodded.

'Say more...'

'Okay, here's what I'm seeing, Eric. Your parents loved you very much yet didn't have all the tools that would have been useful when they were raising you. They were busy at work, immigrants navigating a new country and a new language, and were determined to create security for themselves and their young family. You were the eldest and they assumed you would take responsibility for your younger siblings. However, you were a bright, sensitive child and could have done with something different to really thrive.'

He nodded. 'Yup, not my fault, not their fault, and it happened.'

'Exactly' I replied. 'Great mantra for navigating difficult moments.'

I continued. 'Inevitably, amid the chaos of family

life and absence due to work, you learned they were not reliable, not available. Unable to trust they would be there – that they loved you, you were loveable, worth connecting with and so on – you learned not to trust. You learned love can't be earned. That love is difficult, that relationships are difficult, and somewhere in there you also began to believe there was something wrong with you, some deeply rooted flaw, making you bad and wrong and unloveable.'

His eyes began to fill with tears. We paused, loitering in the sense of it all. Beyond understanding and insight, something different was happening here. I'd been able to get out of my own (professional) way, finding the place in me that holds similar history: bad, wrong, flawed, unloveable. As I was experiencing and in some way sharing/showing this with him, Eric was able to get out of his own way and the space opened. The pause gave us an opportunity to connect in a different way, somehow allowing something greater than both of us to be present for what was unfolding.

And then the moment passed. Internal long-standing mechanisms reorganised him into the bright, intelligent, thinking being, a deeply familiar place where he spends much time. He nodded. 'Go on, I really want to get my head around this.'

'I'm describing the perfect set up for shame. Shame comes from a tear in the fabric of trust. And when shame is magnified by the resulting internal sense of rejection and abandonment, feeling different and misunderstood, we withdraw from connection even further. The further away we withdraw from connection the harder it is to self-soothe, and the more likely we are to search outside for things to make us feel better. Alcohol works well, so does marijuana and sugar, tobacco, gambling, sex – anything with a compulsive element taking us away from the present, away from connection, swirling us further away until we're heading deep into oblivion.'

I paused, aware of how much I had said. 'That was a lot to take in. I'll pause here.'

Big pause.

'Mmmmm.' We waited in companionable silence. I observed the metaphorical cogs whirring in his head as he explored, considered, pondered, sized all this up for usefulness and relevance. I also observed his breath. Sometimes shallow, sometimes expansive, I unconsciously tracked shifts in regularity and depth, matching them with micro-muscle movements in his face, shoulders, belly, hands and feet. I metaphorically sat alongside him, being a companion with no agenda, lots of space, care and concern. The moment was ripe for agape to flow. And then the moment was gone again, broken by his withdrawal to the intellect, trying to figure it all out.

'You know,' he began, 'they told me not to suck my thumb because I wasn't a baby any more. It's one of those moments burned into my memory. I can tell you where

I was, who told me, their tone of voice, what colour the wallpaper was. I didn't know what to do. My thumb was my best friend! Always there!'

I nodded, understanding only too well.

'Later on, there were chocolate cigarettes wrapped in sugar paper and I pretended to smoke like all the grownups around me, sucking and pretending to blow smoke. When I managed to get my hands on real cigarettes, well, I was smitten. Felt really grown up. I remember thinking "I'll show you". And I did. Because then I found dope and it worked a whole lot better than tobacco.'

He paused again, recollecting all the years of sneaking around to get it, rolling joints, toking in secret places with his buddies. An almost imperceptible shudder coursed through his body. Another companionable silence. I instinctively knew to get out of the way, accessing similar experiences – not in a remembering way with thoughts and timelines, but in the way that comes from dipping into the felt sense of it all. Feeling where my body held memories and shame of similar experiences. Allowing vulnerability to emerge. Allowing whatever has taken care of me all these years to present in the space between us. Was something divine manifesting there? Don't know. But I can say there was love again. That sense of agape. And the moment ended, as I knew it would.

'I didn't actually like beer in the beginning. Kinda

liked the effect a whole lot, but not the taste. Then I started raiding their liquor cabinet for the fine stuff – brandy, scotch, port, liqueurs. I especially liked the sweet stuff, you know, Kalhua, Bailey's Irish Cream...' He wandered off into another reverie of memories. I waited. The pause providing companionable space for a felt sense of it all to emerge, in between the tumbling thoughts and insights fighting for their own space in his mind.

'Geez,' he continued, eyes coming to meet mine again. 'It all makes sense now. I never saw all the puzzle pieces fit together like this before. They loved me but I felt unloved. I felt bad and wrong – you're calling that shame – and because I didn't know how to self-soothe or connect with the very people I was supposed to be able to trust, I found solace in things outside of me. Not people, because they were too unpredictable and difficult. Dope and booze have been my best friends for a really long time. Trouble is, no pun intended, they get me into trouble. They get me into trouble because I can't connect with myself or other people when I'm so focused on getting high.'

I nodded slowly, hoping it came across as a mix of understanding and encouragement. Another small pause, creating more room for all this to land and unfold.

'Well, I ain't willing to quit, but I am willing to figure out how to change things. And that's where you can help, right?'

'Yes, Eric, that's where I come in. That is certainly where I can help.'

And our work begins in earnest.

You may think we were at the beginning. Actually, this exchange is drawn from a session years after we began. There had been breaks along the way, some brief and some sustained, and this was the light-bulb moment when Eric had the kind of profound insight shifting something deep enough to make a difference. *Insight accompanied by the felt sense.* I could not have predicted the confluence of events in my life, in his life, that would bring us to this moment, I was just grateful and delighted it had finally arrived.

What I know for sure is that working with the trauma-shame-addiction trilogy provides tough terrain. I've worked with more clients having this condition over the years than I can count. They have had similarities, yet have all been distinct individuals requiring an approach to recovery reflecting their uniqueness. No cookie-cutter approach has ever worked; each client has required precise support and guidance. Interventions must reflect the particular blend of trauma-shame-addiction they bring – for some people trauma will be the lead, for others shame will be louder, for others addiction will be the loudest. The threads are bound so tightly they create a fabric of their own and can no longer be separated. As with Bill.

Waiting in Palo Alto

Eric is one of the people who comes to mind when I reflect on Dorthy's prescient 'There are people waiting for you.' Perhaps inevitably, reflecting my own history, those who stand out are the ones sharing the trauma-shame-addiction shaping. Clearly, in such cases, my attunement would go beyond professional empathy, taking me into such familiar personal healing territory that I could get out of my own way, get out of theirs, and somehow create a different space for them to step into. It's in that pause, in the precious space between us – between words, between stories – that something else can emerge. Whether we call it spirit or grace or intuition, a felt sense of it all manifests. This is what Gene Gendlin talks about in his body of work called focusing.

I may have left Bill behind in SLO, but I soon found a cast of characters in Palo Alto who also seemed bound to find me. Would they evoke the deep sense of connection Bill and I experienced? Would there be love?

Love and Change

Love changes us; lack of love changes us – somehow, even before all the neuroscience research offered proof, we instinctively know this to be so.

I've always known the single most significant element

shaping my life has been the lack of love I experienced growing up. Neither parent was blessed with natural abilities in that department, both tending towards the narcissistic. Fortunately there were other benign and loving influences in the environment around me. However, the result has been not just a requirement but a deep need for the kind of reparative attention denied at the outset. After a false start with my college therapist, the Freudian blank-screen one, I'm grateful for other practitioners rooted in presence and healing.

In recent years I have been moving deeper into the inquiry of focusing, becoming certified as a practitioner in 2018. I've learned so much about how to *do it*, how to *be it*, witnessing clients change. And I have marvelled at this new possibility: without early experience of limbic resonance, I've nevertheless developed competence to provide a safe space for others to step into and experience healing. I don't say this to brag, but to acknowledge that both the client and the practitioner are changed.

In a 1981 interview Gendlin said:

> We just really became much more human and I'm quite sure, I wrote that somewhere, that *we* changed, there is no question about [it]. Now whether the patients changed, we needed to do a lot of research to establish. But we certainly changed.[24]

He's describing a time when, between 1958 and 1963, he was the research director of the Wisconsin study on client-centred therapy with schizophrenics. He talks about becoming more *real as a person* in the face of those who sensed others' reactions more quickly than most; he talks about becoming *looser* and *giving up on formalities*, in the way we have to when working with children. There's a requirement for something inherently more real, immediate, an unavoidable call to authenticity and integrity: that my outsides reflect my insides; that I'm telling the truth.

Why is this so important? It's important to me because acknowledging that love has a role to play in my work transforms how I show up, the kind of supportive supervision I need, the essential nature of continuing to do my own work and engage in self-care. I can't show up to a client session sleep-deprived, hurried, harried and late, discombobulated and discontent and expect to be present in the way they need me to be. I'm reminded of a time when I turned up for therapy with a therapist with whom I was engaged in long-term reparative work. She'd had a significant surgery and, in my opinion, returned to work too soon. She looked pale and frail and for the first time in our years together, I caught her apparently nodding off. In that moment, I had no ability to say anything, yet the experience was wounding. I'm guessing a child-part felt rejected and unloved when usually she felt love and acceptance. It's an extreme example, yet somehow really highlights the value of being at the other end of the scale – open, available, real, connected.

Carol Nickerson, a psychotherapist in California, has written an excellent paper on the importance of attachment, neuroscience and presence in *The Folio*, 2012.[25] She quotes the giants in the attachment field: Bowlby, Winnicott, Schore, Cozolino and Seigel. Here's an excerpt about the value of focusing:

> The process and practice of Focusing embodies the original growth-producing ingredients of brain development: namely, the ingredients that grow within the attachment relationship. Theory and research supports that it is the trust and acceptance within the client-psychotherapist relationship that makes therapy work, regardless of the clinical method. In a review of hundreds of studies examining the outcome of psychotherapy, Orlinsky and Howard (1986) looked for those factors that seemed to relate to success. They found that the quality of the emotional connection between patient and therapist was far more important than the therapist's theoretical orientation.

> Preparing our minds to hold the fullness of another's experience may be the most important aspect of our ongoing training as therapists. (Bodenoch, p.5).

In Cozolino's review of the research on attachment, he states:

> Each parent's unconscious plays a role in the creation of the child's brain, just as the therapist's unconscious contributes to the context and outcome of therapy. This underscores the importance of proper training and adequate personal therapy for therapists, who will be putting their imprint on the hearts, minds, and brains of their clients. (p. 30).

Few places in clinical literature use the word *love*. Even when we all know it's not sexual love but agape, the word is so loaded and open to misinterpretation that most clinicians simply avoid using it at all.

One exception is in Dr. Neil Friedman in his book *Focusing Oriented Therapy*. Just thirty pages in he says:

> Gendlin says that the therapist-client relationship is of first importance, but I do

not think that the word 'love' appears in his index. (I just checked. It doesn't.) ... The therapist needs to cherish, to prize, to love the client. The client needs to feel loved. Not, of course, in the romantic sense. I am talking *agape* here, not *eros*.

I checked as well and concur with Neil; the web as yet reveals no mention by Gendlin of love in this context. He continues:

Of course, seldom do we find the therapist who can live up to such an ideal. I do not. Not by a long shot. I can come to love most clients ('the person in there'). It is better to turn some people away... Maybe love is not enough... but it sure goes a long way.

I found Neil's writing refreshing. Vulnerable, revealing, authentic – it was easy to imagine him as a *shaky being*[26] with his clients. I appreciate him saying, 'It is better to turn some people away' and for that very reason I offer 'chemistry' sessions to potential new clients to get a felt sense of who they are and whether we are a good fit. If I'm honest, a part is checking to see if I can love the person in there. Some are easier than others. Sometimes a client will be better served by someone else. For as Neil concludes: '[therapy] needs to be undertaken in a spirit of unconditional love for "the person in there".'

It was easier for me to love some clients, or at least their loveable parts, than to love others. I worked with many clients over the years in the Bay Area, and some stand out. They are memorable for one reason: there was love in the room. In the synergy we experienced together, love suffused the space between us. And maybe something else as well. I've come to believe love opens the way for an intangible, hard-to-describe, transformative process. What to call this? Perhaps it's spirit, or grace, or intuition; for some it will be closer to God and religion. Whatever the right words are for you, pausing and opening the space for something greater to emerge underpins transformation.

Love and Spirit

Revisiting the bodywork session with Bill all those years ago, it's clear that something to do with spirit, spiritual energy or spiritual presence was at work in the room. While part of me feels uncomfortable with the language, I have a sense there's something absolutely essential about finding a way to talk about it. I share without desire to persuade anyone it's an essential element. For some it may well be, for others perhaps not.

Let's be clear – my own experiences of whatever-this-is that's so hard to describe is fleeting at best, not exactly an everyday occurrence, yet when whatever-this-is presences itself, it's remarkable. As with Bill, when he began to pray in the face of the eerie odour filling the room, something was transformed and we began to find our way through the calamity, out to the other side where hope lived. We did it together, even though he was the initiator and source of the intervention. And some would say he was guided by something else – his belief in God and the divine, a guardian angel, a sense of a power greater than him, or us, guiding to somewhere safe beyond the swamp. My experience that day remains unique, although I've had some other remarkable moments over the years. Moments I don't know how to create deliberately, they come when they come and they don't when they don't – like love, sometimes there it is and other times, simply absent.

I come back to Gendlin's fundamental question about what is most likely to create the space for living forward energy to unfold. And I've become convinced that for some people, some times, a sense of spirit gently emerges and facilitates the way forward. This power greater than ourselves is called many things: Higher Power, God of our understanding, Allah, Yahweh, the Buddha, Muhammad, Jesus, Confucius, etc. My yoga friend speaks of the divine feminine, another friend references the power of the universe. To each their own. That of which I speak may be called by these names, or something else, yet those of us who have a sense of whatever-it-is (I'm going to call it spirit) have a clear knowing of its presence. My hunch is that others, like me, may not know how to summon it; some do seem to have that ability.

The moments I've referred to have come randomly, infrequently and spine-tinglingly disappear as fast as they arrived. What they have in common is a sense of words coming out of my mouth that aren't mine, as if I'm channelling some wisdom I don't own – but only in retrospect. In the moment of delivery I'm simply saying what needs to be said. There's a clarity that no other words will do, these are perfect for the job, they are not mine, they emanate from some greater source than my intellect and experience. As if I've really truly utterly got my Self out of the way and become open to something else guiding. In these moments I don't feel like a *shaky being*, rather a conduit for the God of my understanding, or perhaps my client's. I wish I could remember an example but almost by definition, they only exist in the moment and are soon washed away, leaving only a trace, like the eddy around a seashell in the sand as the tide recedes.

Anticipating this section on Love and Spirit I was expecting to mostly write about that 'still, small voice within' and for me that's a related but different experience. More like listening deeply to a client and having some-thing from my toolbox tug on my sleeve – begging me to mention the book or the TED talk or a suggestion for action – and pausing to listen internally to the soft and gentle 'no' or 'not now' that would get in the way of their process rather than enhance. That feels like spirit taking care of me and us as well, and is different to those other forgotten times I've just described.

Much has been written about listening to that still, small voice within. I continue with one of my favourite quotes, from Judy Moore:

> Gendlin (1964)[27] speculates that focusing 'may be what has always been meant in religious terms by 'listening to the still small voice'' (p. 125) (a phrase familiar to Jewish and Christian religious spiritual traditions originating from the Hebrew Bible: 1 Kings 19:12).[28]

She goes on to explain, so eloquently:

> Listening to the still small voice may be regarded as a deep aspect of congruence or it may be regarded as intuition... Congruence, unconditional positive regard, empathy, contact and perception are all present; but so are presence (Rogers, 1980; Natiello, 2001; Moore, 2001; Geller and

Greenberg, 2002), tenderness (Thorne, 1985), intuition (Bowen, 1986), and openness to divine love (Thorne, 1991a, 1991b, 2002, 2003). It was clear to the older Carl Rogers that listening to all parts of the self, including dreams and bodily sensations, is important for human development. In his late paper 'Aspects of a Person-Centered Approach', Rogers points to the ideal of a highly self-aware person being:

"more potentially aware, not only of the stimuli from outside, but of ideas and dreams, and of the ongoing flow of feelings, emotions and *physiological reactions that he or she senses from within.* The greater this awareness, the more surely the person will float *in a direction consonant with the directional evolutionary flow.*" (1980, pp. 127–128; my emphasis)

Conclusions

Decades into sobriety and my professional practice as a psychotherapist, I have come to believe that *who I am* and therefore *what I embody* is what matters. My toolkit is well equipped. Yet getting out of the way of our natural tendency to heal – providing a nurturing, safe space, sometimes a guiding hand – that's what best facilitates evolution. While I know I made a difference to Bill there are times when part of me wishes I'd been able to bring him this assuredness. And we each did our best.

CHAPTER FIVE

Seeing Bill Again

SETTING UP A CLINICAL PRACTICE IN THE BAY AREA in the early 2000s may not have been advisable on paper. The collapse of the dot.com bubble in 2001 preceded a financial recession, with investors moving their funds, a fall in stock prices, and the kind of clients I worked with finding themselves in surprising difficulty. In fact, some of those consulting me were doing so as a direct result of their resources dwindling from seven figures to six, or even five, overnight. Incredibly stressful times. Achieving work-life balance was a consistent goal, and the coaching side of my practice assisted those willing to embrace the profound changes that goal required. And the more therapeutic side of my practice continued to support those who used alcohol and other substances to manage their distress.

The early 2000s were abundant in learning and personal reward. As Dorthy had foreseen, I had no shortage of clients despite the economic downturn. I was even compelled to create the occasional waiting list. I was also busy pursuing ongoing training with the Strozzi Institute, regularly making the now much shorter round trip from south of the Bay to north of the Bay, with eager anticipation. In parallel, author of *The Survivors Guide to Sex*, Staci K. Haines offered first a beta *Somatics & Trauma* course followed by full-blown trainings, Beginning and Advanced. I attended for four years across all levels. I also had the opportunity to hear speakers such as Dr Stanley Keleman, author of *Emotional Anatomy*, Dr Bessel van der Kolk, author of *The Body Keeps the Score: Brain, Mind, and Body in the Healing of Trauma*, and Dr Pat Ogden, author of *Trauma and the Body: A Sensorimotor Approach to Psychotherapy*. And even Ronald Reagan's son interviewing Mikhail Gorbachev, author Toni Morrison (whose quote 'If there is a book that you want to read, but it hasn't been written yet, you must be the one to write it' inspires me), and the first man on the moon, Neil Armstrong. Abundance indeed.

Along the way Dr Richard Strozzi-Heckler invited me to submit a chapter to his latest offering, an anthology entitled *Being Human at Work: Bringing Somatic Intelligence into Your Professional Life* (North Atlantic Books). My chapter was entitled *The Power of Somatics in Sobriety* (written under my maiden name J. Clare Bowen-Davies) and drew on my work with Bill and others in San Luis Obispo. (Bill appears there as *Jim.*)

Its publication in October 2004 provided the perfect excuse to contact Bill. It had been a couple of years since our final session and I sent him a copy of the book, appreciating all I'd learned from him and wondering if he might be open to meeting for a follow-up session? He agreed, and we arranged to meet some months later in May 2005. I approached the clinician who'd taken over my office in SLO and asked if I could rent it for the occasion, hoping to provide a continued, familiar, safe place for our conversation.

I had never contacted a client after completing treatment with them in this way before and felt concerned about the ethics, the boundaries, the appropriateness of our meeting. I was clear about my professional intention: explore the possibility of collaborating with this man who'd opened my eyes to the complexities of the trauma-shame-addiction triad, perhaps writing something together, and to satisfy my curiosity about how he'd fared since my departure. Personally, my intention was trickier – I felt indebted to Bill yet knew I would never be able to share this delicate piece of information with him. That kind of self-disclosure was beyond my comfort level.

I anticipated the meeting with excitement and nervousness. I remained fond of him, cared about how he was doing, wondered about his health, his sobriety, what he'd say to some kind of professional collaboration – shifting us into unknown territory. Turns out we were both nervous, dancing through the ritual greetings with a lightheartedness belying the butterflies. I asked if I could record the session, something I'd never done before, and I will be forever grateful he agreed. Throughout this whole writing process, whenever I felt stalled or blocked or afraid, I'd listen to his voice and settle myself into recapturing the determination we both had to tell his story.

What follows therefore doesn't rely on memory, glossy or otherwise. What follows is drawn from the undeniable recording of our conversation.

Friday May 13th, 2005 – 3:30pm

There was good news and bad news. The good news: Bill was sober, the business was doing better than ever, he loved living alone in a remote part of the county with his two cats, and he felt calmer and more relaxed than he could have imagined given the rest of the news. The bad news: he was out of remission and beginning chemotherapy again. Even that had its blessing – his sense of a shortened lifespan created an impetus to get his business affairs in order and meant he cherished every single day. Seeing an ending, although not coming soon, gave him comfort that now he could commit to doing things 'right'. He reported being amazed to feel such calm acceptance.

I had incredibly mixed feelings as he relayed his update. I felt sad about the cancer returning yet impressed and proud of the way he was conducting himself amidst it all. I felt bizarrely encouraged, and yet there was something about his calm acceptance that suggested the deep work we'd done, and perhaps which he'd continued with Marie, was inspiring his attitude. I hoped so.

I enquired about Marie and he acknowledged that he'd used her support intermittently, never quite feeling the same connection: 'Honestly,' he said, 'I've always felt the most connection with you... I do remember with you that emotions would come out of nowhere – don't have to know where they came from, they just come from a spark, something gets released, brought up to the surface and I think that had a ton to do with how I feel now.'

I always wondered if my experience of agape came from my imagination, or was it real? With these words, I allowed myself to acknowledge I hadn't made it up, that indeed the feeling was mutual.

Reflection continued, Bill contemplating the weird and wonderful bodywork session I described in our work together, truly the pivotal moment that permitted a sense of there being something bigger than both of us supporting our work together. I recalled a session when he reported gold balls of light swirling inside his torso and chest, allowing a spiritual connection which brought healing, loving energy. 'You're the only one that's done that with me, you recommended a bodywork gal, but she didn't know how to do what you did, haven't been able to get the same kind of treatment,' he said. 'I'd never know what to expect [with bodywork] and sometimes there'd be a lot and sometimes nothing and sometimes I'd cry, sometimes I'd be bawling, don't know where that came from.'

We pondered the trauma, drawing on Dr Bessel van der Kolk's work suggesting that trauma is stored at cellular level. 'There was a lot from Vietnam,' he continued. 'I don't know how much from childhood, hard to know... we talked about my first tour of Vietnam... I remember so little... and that it wasn't necessarily important that I remembered, but a lot of it came out in the bodywork sessions because intellectually I couldn't remember.' He went on to say 'there were flashes of things... there's probably more, but the most important things came out.'

If ever a testimonial were needed for the value of hands-on bodywork in such scenarios, here it was. I felt enormous gratitude for all I'd learned with Dr Richard Strozzi-Heckler and Staci K. Haines, for they were committed – and remain so – to hands-on bodywork forming part of the strategy for resolving trauma. There's something unique about the kind of relationship established when touch is involved. A deeper layer of trust somehow, a more profound level of relationship – non-sexual, caring and healing. And since trauma happens in relationship, I firmly believe it can only be healed *in relationship*. Hence the necessity for the practitioner to be present, empathically attuned and offering the unconditional positive regard prescribed by the father of counselling, Carl Rogers.

Bill went on to describe how he viewed our work together. 'In my mind there were three things: psycho-therapy, bodywork and the third part was kinda spiritual, hard to describe.' He continued, 'Hard to really name because in the naming of it, it changes… it's something more meaningful, something bigger than us.' Even as I type these words, I smile. I love him saying 'in the naming of it, it changes.' For that's my experience as well. Finding the words to reveal the depths is beyond challenging.

Our conversation continued, gently drifting back and forth and into the nooks and crannies of his life two years after our final session. He described living in a remote location without a mail box and only his cats for company, quickly adding how comforting this was for him. Reflecting his sensitivity and desire for a significant amount of recharging alone time, he also knew this could be problematic – alone is different from lonely. He was in touch with a few close friends, some acquaintances from a sober group he'd attended, and got the most joy from being with his team at work. He spoke of them proudly, as if they were children, and in a way they were family.

I noticed a greater comfort as he spoke of those dear to him. As if he inhabited all of his body to its edges, not just the core and a little bit beyond. His face relaxed, he smiled and settled more into the chair, hands becoming calmer in his lap. There was a sigh, some space, and we sat contentedly in the companionable silence just as we used to. He seemed to drift, a softer, faraway look in his eyes, and I became aware of how that companionable silence had served us before. A way to invite something greater than us to be present. I relaxed and took a deep breath as well. Forever influencing one another, the natural ebb and flow between us opened another possibility for our connection and conversation.

His reverie came to an end, he looked at me shyly and went on:

> I wish there was a way to quantify what we did and how much it helped me because I know it did me a ton of good and I don't know how to put that into words.

Another pause, then he continued:

> The part you brought in was the actual physical part of the body. That's something I never would have thought of on my own. I wouldn't have thought a spiritual

connection was there. Guess it's that place
inside me that always knows what's right.

The word *namaste* came to mind. I glanced at the place
on the wall where my *Namaste* poster used to hang.
Beautifully penned by a grateful client on her departure,
it had always held a treasured place in the room.

NAMASTÉ

I honor the place in you in which the
    entire universe dwells.
I honor the place in you which is of love,
    of truth, of light, and of peace.
When you are in the place in you and I am
    in that place in me, we are one.

I doubt Bill had ever come across *namaste*. As a Christian
who didn't divert much from traditional sources, it's not
a word we ever used, yet I thought how aptly it described
'in the naming of it, it changes'. I'm certain that on the
day of our momentous bodywork session there was
something of spirituality, inner wisdom and grace in the
room with us.

From here we talked about his drift from AA,
remaining somewhat active and having a sponsor, yet not
following a predictable schedule of attendance. Part of

me felt concerned, knowing his tendency to isolate, yet I trusted that inner wisdom he just mentioned – with some consistent sobriety under his belt now, he now had a sense of purpose and connection with the God of his understanding on which to rely.

A little selfishly, I asked what he could do now that he couldn't do back when we started our work. Grounding and centring wasn't routine, yet he acknowledged how satisfied he felt having navigated some stressful business meetings with the type of people who wear collar and tie in comparison to his work overalls, immediately intimidating. He may not have grounded himself in the classic sense yet he had remembered to take a deep breath, all the way down in to his belly, and that settled his anxiety:

> When I make a big decision or something
> I usually say a little prayer, relax a little bit,
> think about the decision, not all the time,
> but sometimes I remember oh that's when
> Clare said it would be good to centre and
> feel my belly.

Faced with the temptation of 'liquor alley' in the grocery store, Bill remembered how it was:

> When I'm distracted the bottle sort of
> leaps into my cart, I end up going out the

door with it, that's the way I remember it.
Even though I know what I'm doing...
something inside me is saying no no
no, but it wasn't strong enough or loud
enough... so I am totally disconnected
from myself.

These days, he reported: 'Here's exactly the thought that
goes through my mind: there's absolutely no positive part
to having a drink.' And with that clear intention and a
deep breath or two, he's able to avoid the liquor aisles,
treating them as if they don't exist. What a difference.

Our time began to come to a natural close and as we
began to wrap up, Bill said:

I wish more people were doing what you
did... I'm glad you're writing about it,
people will be interested.

Every time fear gets in the way of writing our story,
whenever I can't imagine a single person wanting to read
any of this, I reflect on his encouragement. As someone
dear to me said recently, in words reminiscent of Dorthy,
'There are people waiting for your book.'

CHAPTER SIX

My Love

THE ONE WASN'T WAITING FOR ME IN THE BAY AREA after all. But I needed to kiss one last frog there, someone who would inadvertently lead me to the love of my life.

Something about Bart drew me in, yet something also repelled me. He was older, wiser, protective and paternal, yet underneath brewed layers of abandonment, rejection and rage. A divorced father of grown-up children, he confused me: a charming bon vivant who could be lavish and generous one minute, budgeting and spending on a shoestring the next. He swerved between gentle attentiveness and clumsy controlling behaviour. I found myself overriding these early instinctive red light warnings, agreeing to more time together.

The details of our two years together are too painful

(and embarrassing) to recount. It wasn't until the end drew nigh, when my/our therapist confronted his alcoholism that the penny dropped. Here I was, a recovering alcoholic with nearly fifteen years sobriety, dutifully standing by (as only a co-dependent can), refusing to acknowledge that those initial signals were valid. *An alcoholic?* I'd allowed his epicurean taste for the finest of food and wine to take me in completely. Alcohol is alcohol is alcohol – I knew better than regard those good old excuses of 'I only drink beer, never spirits' or 'I never drink in the mornings'. I had been partnering with an alcoholic all this time and I was stunned. Mortified as well. The realisation paved the way to yet more self-exploration and healing, preparing me for what was to come.

Paul was around the corner: my kindergarten buddy, already wielding spanners and changing tyres under his father's tutelage.

Remember Me?

It was July 2005, and an email arrived from friends-reunited.co.uk.

'Remember me?' the message said. 'The one who poked you in the eye?'

I had the vaguest of memories of being poked in the eye – given its relatively traumatic nature – but my heart skipped several beats when I saw the name at the bottom of the message. Paul Myatt. Oh my word, here was my best friend from kindergarten and beyond. We hadn't been in contact for twenty-six years.

Being poked in the eye may not seem a propitious start, yet this sums up Paul's playfulness and sense of humour.

In kindergarten – for this is the scene of the crime – we lay down in small beds after lunch for a nap and he generally chose the one next to me. I have to say, I was oblivious to this. Kindergarten began as a nightmare for me as an only child, a sensitive child, who didn't know how to interact with other small people, having had little exposure to them before arriving just turned four to a room full of them. As an energetic three-year-old, someone who could get around any room without touching the floor (imagine: furniture, curtains, people...), Paul didn't enjoy these nap times and wanted to play. Ready for mischief one day, he tried opening my eyes with his fingers. This didn't go well. My wails being proof. I must admit I have little recollection of the incident in question, Paul remembers because he got into trouble, a commonplace occurrence for this little rascal.

A Phone Call

He sounded just like I remembered. Soft, gentle, with love and care. And tons of humour. (One of the first poems he sent me was Spike Milligan's *British Teeth*, not exactly your classic romantic outpouring, yet true to who he is.) After the awkward niceties, I came to understand how often he'd thought of me. He was delighted to find I was single, although living in California came as a bit of a shock. He'd visited the East Coast before but never the West; realisation dawned just how far apart we lived.

We soon got into a rhythm of twice daily contact, bookending our days. As I was getting up, he was coming to the end of his workday so I'd hear how things had gone and he'd wish me well for mine; as I went to bed, he was getting up the following morning, so time for another check in. We rarely missed a day and there was so much to talk about. Twenty-six years to catch up on, as well as the times we'd spent together as youngsters. Reminiscing about our friendship, being boyfriend-girlfriend for a while around the twenty-one mark, there was a lot of ground to cover.

Meeting

As our connection renewed and deepened, talk turned to meeting up. It would be the first time since the late 1970s, when we both had slender waists and perms. (Although Paul would prefer I didn't mention this, he's thoroughly embarrassed about the hairdo.) Paul had never been to the West Coast and was curious about glowing stories of my life there, yet his mother was sick and we determined I'd fly to the UK for the reunion. As I sat in LAX Airport, journalling furiously – will he? won't he? – little did I know dear Thelma was taking her last breaths. Surrounded by her loving family, she passed on the very day I was getting on the plane. Knowing her demise to be imminent, he'd confided his heart to her and she made him promise he would meet me at the airport and carry on with his plans. Ever the generous one.

Emerging through the final gate, I saw him straight away, little changed over the years. Well, that's not strictly true, but in my mind's eye he was the cheeky chappie I remembered from our young adulthood. Blonde, blue eyed, with a grin spread from ear to ear. In the best movies, this is where time slows, hearts pound, desire builds. Yes, there was all of that. And behind the smiling eyes, profound sadness at being so newly orphaned.

In all honesty, looking back I have to acknowledge I was pretty oblivious to the distress. I was so thrilled to be reunited, ecstatic at the prospect of being together after all our conversations, I didn't understand the depth of his loss. Not until the first of my parents died did I truly realise the extent of my unmindful chatter that day. And somehow he was able to compartmentalise the sadness, focused as he was on fulfilling the promise to his mother and sharing my excitement.

Nordy Bank

We spent the next few days like a couple of teenagers, visiting old haunts in London before driving to Brugges for a romantic weekend. Mid-December, we had no idea just how cold it would be in that beautiful city, lurching from one cafe to the next for steaming mugs of hot chocolate to thaw out frozen fingers, toes and faces. Our revelry was cut short though; we needed to return for the funeral. A close-knit family, Paul's sisters put on a brave face and made the best of an enormously difficult time.

The following day was Christmas-Eve-eve. A chilly but sunny day, we left his sister's house to explore the area, one unfamiliar to me. Beautiful rolling hills and a wintry landscape unfolded as we drove deeper into the country-side. Paul showed me the sixteenth century cottage he'd renovated in a nearby yet remote village. We drove some more, all the time holding hands and learning more about one another. A five-barred gate and hillside beckoned and we began climbing to the top of an Iron Fort, a Roman lookout from long ago. Catching our breath, we looked out over the Shropshire scenery, admiring the terrain. Aware of something shifting, I found Paul down in the grass and the light began to dawn – he was down on one knee. OMG. He asked those words I'd been longing to hear and I remember saying, 'I'd be delighted.'

Something about sharing the momentous news

gripped us both, but with no phone signal atop the hill, and in the age of pre-texting, we stood together like a couple of grinning adolescents wanting to shout our good news to the sky. We didn't have long to wait. As if by a miracle, we saw a ghostly figure approaching us along the top of Nordy Bank, literally emerging through the low cloud. We told him! And I asked if he'd take a photo, the first of us betrothed. He obliged. The sheep looked on without interest, then he disappeared into the ether, as effortlessly as he'd arrived.

Being smart, my new fiancé hadn't chosen a ring yet, giving me the option of selecting exactly the right one. Which I did, post-haste, in time to meet the family over Christmas and share our news.

Decision time

I was all loved up and on cloud nine, but the time came to return to California. There were tears, on both sides, for having found one another again parting was a wrench. But that was inevitable, just as the decision about who was going to move. At some level we both knew, even then, that I would be moving back to the UK. Not only did Paul have family and business ties, to say nothing of several Jaguar XKs from the 1950s ready to be restored, moving to the UK would also provide the possibility for healing my family wounds.

So we endured six months apart before I returned

in July 2006 in time for our 9 September wedding. Another private practice to close and any amount of prior experience didn't make it any easier. I didn't have someone like Bill to have closure with, but a group of committed clients, some long-term, who I knew would be disappointed and pleased for me, in equal measure. I began the challenging task of closure with my clients, packing up my home, and leaving my beloved cats with friends. When this comes up, my love is likely to have a boyish smile and say, 'But I'm worth it.' Indeed he is.

EPILOGUE

Visiting Bill

THE STRETCH OF HIGHWAY 101 BETWEEN SAN LUIS
Obispo and San Francisco is as familiar to me as the
shape of the wedding and engagement rings now
adorning my left hand. They're curved, fitting neatly
together like a couple spooning. There's comfort in
looking at them, the stones shining in the California sun-
light. The Central Coast approached. Beyond King City,
I knew San Miguel would be next, then Paso Robles and
finally today's destination: Atascadero. Some of the locals
irreverently call it A-trash-cadero. An undeserved name,
especially nowadays with its renovated downtown, quaint
coffee shops and gift stores to left and right. My heart
skipped a beat. A step closer.

The wonder of the internet meant finding the address

for his engineering company had been easy. Would he be there? Calling ahead seemed too weird for words, so the decision had been made to nonchalantly stop by and enquire. Nonchalant. Well, hardly. I wanted the visit to seem nonchalant but it felt anything but. So much water had passed under the proverbial bridge – for me, for him – how would it be to see him again? I had already rehearsed what I was going to say but I also knew better than to think this would be available to me with anxiety coursing through my body. And I was definitely feeling more and more anxious as the freeway exit approached. I knew exactly where it was, had taken it a thousand times, but not for the sake of visiting Bill.

Highway 46. Here it was. Our exit. The feeling shifted. A mix of anxiety and excitement, nervous anticipation at what would unfold. 'At the end of the road, turn right,' squawked the GPS. I certainly hadn't been exactly here before. Not even in all my days making home visits for Child Protective Services; two years taking me the length and breadth of the county, searching out abusive parents and attempting to protect their children. My specialty was addiction, so I was assigned the parents who were known to abuse alcohol and other drugs. I came to wonder if there were any other type. Talk about naive. I knew so little, had such high hopes for making a difference, yet only managed to make waves here and there. Turning right, there was the sign. We pulled into the parking lot in front. I noticed the tension holding up my shoulders, tightening my jaw, butterflies fighting for space in my belly. 'We're here,' I said. 'Will you wait for me?' A silly question, yet felt the need to ask.

Paul nodded. He knew better than to engage in conversation. We'd already reviewed the visit, how I wanted it to go, what I hoped for, his role – to stay in the car – and mine, to bravely venture inside and ask the question I'd been waiting years and thousands of miles to ask. He smiled encouragingly, nodding with understanding. 'It's okay, go in.' I nodded in return, a weak smile covering the melee of feelings inside.

I pulled a brush through my hair, rolled my lips, popped a tiny mint and took a deep breath. 'I can do this,' I said to myself in a reassuring voice. 'It's okay.' I looked down at those rings again, a security blanket in many ways, looked once more at Paul and opened the door. The heat of the day hit me forcibly; it was like opening the door to an oven. My feet landed on the ground, warm tarmac seeping through the soles of my shoes, and I turned towards the building. One floor-to-ceiling sliding door was open to the left of reception and I wondered if he could see me walking towards the building. The sun was too bright to see what was inside, just the outlines of men moving bulky equipment around. Was one of them Bill?

The overhanging canopy gave enough shade to see

inside to the front office and I could see a dark-haired woman on the phone. Good, that would buy me a few more moments to compose myself if I had to wait while she finished. Pushing the door open, I walked inside, the air-conditioned cool of the interior a pleasant relief from the sun overhead. Sure enough, one woman wielded a phone in her hand at the front, and another much younger one sat at a desk beyond, working away on a computer. She looked up, her youthful and enquiring face making eye contact.

'Hi there, can I help you?'

'Mmm, yes, I hope so! My name's Clare, I'm an old friend of Bill's. I wonder if he's here today?'

Her face fell, a pallor overtaking her features. I had my answer. The woman in front put her hand over the telephone receiver, catching her junior's eye, saying, 'Who are you again? Who did you say you are?' The dark-haired woman took over; she was clearly in charge here.

'My name's Clare and I used to know Bill years ago, when I lived in SLO. I moved away. I'm back visiting and I just wondered if I could see him...' and now I was stuttering, I knew it was all coming out too fast and high-pitched. 'We've been out of touch for a while and I was in the area and I just really wanted to see him again.' I ended sheepishly, or was it despairingly? I already knew what she was going to say, or at least feared the exact news I was about to hear.

'Gee, I'm so sorry,' she said. 'Bill died in 2008. He had cancer, you know. He was well for a while then It came back.'

I could feel a part of me lifting out of my body to watch this whole ghastly, unreal scene. I went cold, a shiver running from head to foot. It wasn't the air-conditioning. I felt chilled to the bone. I could feel my hands quivering and tears springing. Darn it, no tissues. Oh, don't cry! I swallowed loudly, gulping back everything that wanted to pour forth.

Thoughts screamed through my head, no censor in place 'NO, no, don't say that. I'm too late. Shit. He's gone. I waited too long.' Blaming and shaming. Tears began to prick my eyes, I knew I had to leave before a torrent burst forth. I smiled faintly. 'Oh, gosh, yes I knew about the cancer. I'm really sorry to hear that. Thank you for telling me, thank you.' I think she asked me something else and I don't remember what I said next, so focused was I on escape, just wanting to head back to the security of Paul and our cocoon on wheels.

What is there to say in such circumstances? I had wished for professional composure, poise and grace. I don't think I disgraced myself, but I wasn't proud of running away. I threw myself into the passenger seat. Bursting into tears, no more words necessary. Bill was dead. Too late to say goodbye; thank you and goodbye.

Paul started up the car and pulled away with ease,

allowing my all-consuming grief to fill the space around us. He knew. He didn't need to ask and anyway, I didn't have capacity for words. As we pulled onto the freeway south, his right hand reached for mine – part of me wanted to resist, denying myself the soothing contact. But the healthier part acquiesced, allowing the warmth of the connection to travel up my arm to surround the coldness in my heart. Sobs began to subside. I found tissues and began to mop up the mess. We drove on in companionable silence. Still nothing useful to be said. Deep sadness all-encompassing.

The tears eventually abated, and I felt a settling happening through my body, like tea leaves sinking slowly into a teacup. I looked up and saw the bright blue skies overhead, the sun shining. I glanced across at Paul's profile and catching his eye, he winked. My impish husband knew exactly how to interrupt the flow of my downward spiral and I couldn't help but smile. A watery one, but nevertheless, a small smile. 'Chocolate?' he asked, using one of his funny voices, this time a local accent from home. He'd come prepared, bless him. For of course, chocolate would be my preferred substance of choice at such a time. No longer alcohol, thank God (well, Higher Power actually, but you understand). And I began to drift into a reverie of gratitude. 'There but for the grace of God go I' came to mind. A platitude? Yes and no.

I would never know if Bill had achieved significant abstinence before departing this life and somehow that seemed important. Not as a measure of success – mine or his – but as a way of assessing the quality of his last days. I hope they were alcohol-free. I hope he was surrounded by people who cared for him and that he could feel their care. I hope he didn't suffer. Cancer can be so cruel.

And I thought back over my own life with its twists and turns, many of the most dramatic being here on the Central Coast of California. I'd found recovery from alcoholism in Los Angeles many years before and moved here, deepening into a sober community, working professionally with others who were captured by addiction. In retrospect, my experience in early to middle sobriety reflected much drama, my own and others. I moved further north to the Bay Area, and began to find my feet, intensifying somatic exploration both personally and professionally, taking a deep dive into self-generative healing. All this had prepared me to be reunited with the love of my life, move back to England, and here we sat together now, hand in hand on Highway 101 heading for Avila Beach. Boy was I one lucky, grateful, privileged soul. And that's why I say 'there but for the grace of God go I.' What had me be so fortunate? How did I escape the myriad catastrophes which could have befallen me on the way? Have there always been angels guiding and guarding? And at what point will I be able to acknowledge the immense amount of gut-wrenching personal development work that underpins the quality of my life – yes, I've been blessed, and yes, I've worked my ass off.

We arrived at Sycamore Mineral Springs, one of my favourite places in the world. Private hot tubs, dotted around the hillside wooded areas above Avila Beach, offer naturally heated mineral water bubbling up from the rich earth. Day or night, under clear or rainy skies, there's nowhere I'd rather be. Throughout my SLO days I'd escape to the hot tubs, alone or with select friends, and we'd skinny-dip in the deliciously warm luxury of the water, complete with sulphur aroma and candles if we remembered them. Deep joy.

Whether the meeting I had planned to have with Bill went well or not so well, I had known that it would be important to have something soothing afterwards. This was the perfect choice. And a real reflection of how far I'd come – no longer craving oblivion in a bottle, and with a new capacity for self-respect and self-care. The devastating news of Bill's death and consequent inability to express my profound thanks could have tipped me over the edge, but with expanding self-compassion and the love of my life at my side, I was able to stand my ground. Finally ready to accept Richard's assessment: 'An exemplar of recovery.'

Be Blessed

May you recognise in your life the presence, power and light of your soul.

May you realise that you are never alone, that your soul in its brightness and belonging connects you

intimately with the rhythm of the universe. May you have respect for your individuality and difference.

May you realise that the shape of your soul is unique, that you have a special destiny here,

that behind the facade of your life there is something beautiful, good, and eternal happening.

May you learn to see yourself with the same delight, pride, and expectation with which God sees you in every moment.

– John O'Donohue, in *Anam Cara*

ACKNOWLEDGEMENTS

I AM GRATEFUL TO THE MANY TEACHERS WHO HAVE guided my learning. Special thanks go to Dr Richard Strozzi-Heckler and Staci K. Haines at Strozzi Institute. To CALFAM (California Family Studies Center, now known as Phillips Graduate University) for providing my Marriage and Family Therapist training, and multiple organisations offering internships to hone my early skills. Thanks to Gloria Moore MFT, for support with the gruelling California Marriage and Family Therapist licensing process and Dr Stephanie Brown for robust supervision in Palo Alto. More recently, Jerry Conway, Kay Hoffmann and Dr Ann Weiser Cornell have guided my focusing studies. Thank you, all.

Since the best therapy I've provided most likely

came from the best I received, grateful thanks go to Dr Sheryn T. Scott, Wendy Deaton MFT and Dr Alan G. Tidmarsh.

Gratitude to the many clients whose confidentiality I uphold and who have contributed to me becoming a seasoned practitioner.

To my writer friends and first readers, I thank you for urging me on when I baulked at the task: Angela Dunning, Beverley McMaster, Bob Golling, Eve Menezes Cunningham, Francis Briers, Keren Smedley, Maggie Richards, Nancy Shanteau, Pete Hamill, Dr Sally Austen, Dr Scarlett Heinbuch and Dr Wilson Wall.

To Duncan Lockerbie at Lumphanan Press, gratitude for guiding me through the perilous process of self-publishing.

Many have heard about 'writing the book' for way too long – thanks dear friends for your patience and encouragement: Alison Wall, Bailey Drechsler, Dawn Bentley, Harriet Lavender Brown, Kimberly Sanders Hamilton, Merle McKinley, Sandy Sagraves, Trudy Arthurs and especially Sharon Machrone.

And to my husband Paul, abiding love.

ENDNOTES

Chapter One

1. Dr. Elaine Aron has been researching the Highly Sensitive Person since 1991. For more information see: http://hsperson.com

2. An updated definition of PTSD came into effect in 2013. For details see: https://www.psychiatry.org/psychiatrists/practice/dsm/educational-resources/dsm-5-fact-sheets

3. http://www.avqp-vets.com/vietnam3.html and http://www.avqp-vets.com/PTSD.html

4. https://www.psychiatry.org/psychiatrists/practice/dsm/educational-resources/dsm-5-fact-sheets

5. http://www.publichealth.va.gov/exposures/radiation/diseases.asp and http://www.avqp-vets.com/vietnam3.html

Chapter Two

6. *The Anatomy of Change* by Richard Strozzi-Heckler, Ph.D. explores this process. See: Strozzi-Heckler, Richard, (1997) *Anatomy of Change: A Way To Move Through Life's Transitions.* North Atlantic Books.

7. Although frequently credited to an anonymous Navy Seal, this quote is originally attributed to the Greek lyrical poet, Archilochus.

8. Richard Schmidt and Timothy Lee, *Motor Control and Learning: A Behavioral Emphasis*, Champagne, IL: Human Kinetics, 2011, in *Access to Power* by Julia Kelliher, Chapter 11.
See: Kelliher, Julia; Julia, Carol, and Shanteau, Nancy (2014). *Access to Power: A Radical Approach for Changing Your Life.* Spring Street Press.

9. George Leonard, *Mastery.* See: Leonard, George (1991). *Mastery: The Keys to Success and Long-Term Fulfillment (Plume).* Penguin.

Chapter Three

10. Quoted from Vietnam Veterans and Alcoholism, August 1984 by Thomas Brinson and Vince Treanor: http://archive.vva.org/archive/TheVeteran/2005_03/feature_alcoholism.htm

11. 'Literally, within a brief 24–36-hour period, a combat soldier could be plucked away from his buddies in the middle of a firefight and deposited into the chaos of an urban traffic jam with no accommodations for jet-lag, much less for the culture-shock of readjustment to American life.'

From Vietnam Veterans and Alcoholism, August 1984 by Thomas Brinson and Vince Treanor: http://archive.vva.org/archive/TheVeteran/2005_03/feature_alcoholism.htm

12. 'Boscarino (1981) asserts in his analysis of data collected in 1977 that in-country veterans had substantially higher levels of alcohol consumption and binge-drinking episodes than comparable groups of era veterans and non-veterans.' From Vietnam Veterans and Alcoholism, August 1984 by Thomas Brinson and Vince Treanor: http://archive.vva.org/archive/TheVeteran/2005_03/feature_alcoholism.htm

13. https://www.historynet.com/marine-showdown-at-dai-do-recollections-of-a-green-one-four-man.htm

14. My personal favourite is Andy Puddicombe juggling throughout his TED talk: https://www.ted.com/talks/andy_puddicombe_all_it_takes_is_10_mindful_minutes

15. http://www.smartrecovery.org

16. http://www.sossobriety.org

17. http://www.celebraterecovery.com

18. http://www.womenforsobriety.org

19. http://lifering.org

20. Chlordiazepoxide, trade name Librium, is a sedative and hypnotic medication of the benzodiazepine class; it is used to treat anxiety, insomnia and withdrawal symptoms from

alcohol and/or drug abuse. Chlordiazepoxide has a medium to long half-life but its active metabolite has a very long half-life. (Wikipedia)

21. http://www.ehealthme.com/ds/librium/hallucination

22. Purportedly organised by the US CIA, Phoenix program death squads operated to destroy both civilian administration and infrastructure supporting the VietCong. See https://en.wikipedia.org/wiki/Phoenix_Program

23. http://www.alcoholics-anonymous.org.uk

Chapter Four

24. Gendlin, E.T. and G. Lietaer (1983). 'On client-centered and experiential psychotherapy: an interview with Eugene Gendlin'. In W.R. Minsel and W. Herff (Eds), *Research on psychotherapeutic approaches. Proceedings of the 1st European conference on psychotherapy research, Trier, 1981, Vol. 2*, pp. 77–104. Frankfurt am Main/Bern: Peter Lang. See https://www.focusing.org/gendlin/docs/gol_2102.html

25. Carol Nickerson, 'Attachment And Neuroscience: The Benefits of Being a Focusing Oriented Professional', *The Folio, Volume 23, 2012*. See http://www.focusing.org/folio/Vol23No12012/04_ Nickerson_FocusingResearch.pdf

26. Gendlin, E.T. (1990). 'The small steps of the therapy process: How they come and how to help them come'. In G. Lietaer, J. Rombauts and R. Van Balen (Eds), *Client-centered and*

experiential psychotherapy in the nineties, Leuven: Leuven University Press, pp. 205–224.

The Primacy of Human Presence
by Eugene Gendlin

"I want to start with the most important thing I have to say: the essence of working with another person is to be present as a living being. And this is lucky, because if we had to be smart, or good, or mature, or wise, then we would probably be in trouble. But, what matters is not that. What matters is to be a human being with another human being, to recognize the other person as another being in there. Even if it is a cat or a bird, if you are trying to help a wounded bird, the first thing you have to know is that there is somebody in there, and that you have to wait for that "person," that being in there, to be in contact with you. That seems to me to be the most important thing.

"So; when I sit down with someone, I take my troubles and feelings and I put them over here, on one side, close, because I might need them. I might want to go in there and see something. And I take all the things I have learnt - client-centered therapy, reflection, focusing, gestalt, psycho-analytic concepts and everything else (I wish I had even more) - and I put them over here, on my other side, Close. Then I am just here, with my eyes, and there is this other being. If they happen to look into my eyes, they will see that I am just a shaky being. I have to tolerate that. They may not look. But if they do, they will see that.

They will see the slightly shy, slightly withdrawing insecure existence that I am. I have learnt that that is ok. I do not need to be emotionally secure and firmly present. I just need to be present. There are no qualifications for the kind of person I must be. What is wanted for the big therapy process, the big development process is a person who will be present. And so I have gradually become convinced that even I can be that. Even though I have my doubts when I am by myself, in some objective sense I know I am a person."

From:
https://www.focusing.org/gendlin/docs/gol_2110.html

27. Gendlin, E. T. (1964). 'A Theory of Personality Change'. In P. Worchel and D. Byrne (Eds), *Personality Change.* New York: Wiley, pp. 102–148.

28. Moore, Judy (2003). *Letting Go of Who I Think I Am: Listening to the unconditioned self.* University of East Anglia, Norwich, UK

(all urls correct as of April 2019)

BIBLIOGRAPHY

Alcoholics Anonymous The Big Book, fourth edition (2002). Alcoholics Anonymous World Services.

Aron, Elaine N. (2017). *The Highly Sensitive Person*. Harper Thorsons.

Blake, Amanda (2018). *Your Body Is Your Brain: Leverage Your Somatic Intelligence To Find Purpose, Build Resilience, Deepen Relationships and Lead More Powerfully.* Trokay Press.

Bradshaw, John (2006). *Healing the Shame that Binds You.* Health Communications.

Briere, John (1992). *Child Abuse Trauma: Theory and Treatment of the Lasting Effects (Interpersonal Violence: The Practice Series).* Sage Publications.

Briers, Francis (2014). *My Tao Te Ching - A Fool's Guide to Effing the Ineffable*. Warriors of Love Publishing.

Brown, Brené (2010). *The Gifts of Imperfection: Let Go of Who You Think You're Supposed to Be and Embrace Who You Are*. Hazelden.

Brown, Brené (2015). *Daring Greatly: How the Courage to Be Vulnerable Transforms the Way We Live, Love, Parent, and Lead*. Penguin Life.

Brown, Stephanie (1988). *Treating Adult Children of Alcoholics: A Developmental Perspective (Wiley Series on Personality Processes)*. John Wiley & Sons.

Brown, Stephanie (2008). *Treating the Alcoholic: A Developmental Model of Recovery (Wiley Series on Personality Processes Book 109)*. Wiley-Interscience.

Brown, Stephanie (2012). *The Alcoholic Family in Recovery: A Developmental Model*. The Guilford Press.

Fogel, Alan, (2013). *Body Sense: The Science and Practice of Embodied Self-Awareness (Norton Series on Interpersonal Neurobiology)*. W. W. Norton & Company.

Friedman, Neil (2007). *Focusing-Oriented Therapy*. iUniverse.

Gendlin, Eugene T. (2003). *Focusing: How to Gain Direct Access to Your Body's Knowledge: How to Open Up Your Deeper Feelings and Intuition*. Rider.

Grof, Christina (1994). *The Thirst for Wholeness: Attachment, Addiction and the Spiritual Path*. Bravo Ltd.

Haines, Staci K. (2007). *Healing Sex: A Mind-body Approach to Healing Sexual Trauma.* Cleis Press.

Hamill, Pete (2013). *Embodied Leadership: The Somatic Approach to Developing Your Leadership.* Kogan Page.

Hari, Johann (2016). *Chasing the Scream: The First and Last Days of the War on Drugs.* Bloomsbury Paperbacks.

Heinbuch, Scarlett (2018). *Waking Up To Love: Our Shared-Near Death Encounter Brought Miracles, Recovery and Second Chances.* Waterside Press.

Hendrix, Harville (2005). *Keeping the Love You Find: Single Persons Guide to Achieving Lasting Love.* Simon & Schuster.

Herman, Judith (2015). *Trauma and Recovery: The Aftermath of Violence--From Domestic Abuse to Political Terror.* Basic Books.

Kasl, Charlotte Davis (1992). *Many Roads, One Journey: Moving Beyond the 12 Steps.* HarperPerennial.

Kasl, Charlotte Davis (1990). *Women, Sex And Addiction: A Search For Love and Power.* HarperPerennial.

Keleman, Stanley (1989). *Emotional Anatomy.* Center Press.

Kelliher, Julia; Julia, Carol, and Shanteau, Nancy (2014). *Access to Power: A Radical Approach for Changing Your Life.* Spring Street Press.

Leonard, George (1991). *Mastery: The Keys to Success and Long-Term Fulfillment (Plume).* Penguin.

Levine, Peter (1997). *Waking The Tiger: Healing Trauma – The Innate Capacity to Transform Overwhelming Experiences.* North Atlantic Books.

Levine, Peter (2015). *Trauma and Memory: Brain and Body in a Search for the Living Past: A Practical Guide for Understanding and Working with Traumatic Memory.* North Atlantic Books.

Madison, Greg (2014). *Theory and Practice of Focusing-Oriented Psychapy: Beyond the Talking Cure.* Jessica Kingsley Publishers

Madison, Greg (2014). *Emerging Practice in Focusing-Oriented Psychapy: Innovative Theory and Applications (Advances in Focusing-Oriented Psychotherapy).* Jessica Kingsley Publishers

Maté, Gabor (2018). *In the Realm of Hungry Ghosts: Close Encounters with Addiction.* Vermillion.

Menezes-Cunningham, Eve (2017). *365 Ways to Feel Better: Self-Care Ideas for Embodied Well-Being.* White Owl.

Ogden, Pat and Fisher, Janina (2015). *Sensorimotor Psychotherapy: Interventions for Trauma and Attachment (Norton Series on Interpersonal Neurobiology).* W. W. Norton & Company.

Rothschild, Babette (2000). *The Body Remembers: The Psychophysiology of Trauma and Trauma Treatment.* Norton Professional Books (Hardcover): W. W. Norton & Company.

Scaer, Robert C. (2014). *The Body Bears the Burden: Trauma, Dissociation, and Disease.* Routledge.

Silsbee, Doug, (2008). *Presence-Based Coaching: Cultivating Self-Generative Leaders Through Mind, Body, and Heart.* John Wiley & Sons.

Strozzi-Heckler, Richard (1997) *Anatomy of Change: A Way To Move Through Life's Transitions.* North Atlantic Books.

Strozzi-Heckler, Richard (2004). *Being Human at Work: Bringing Somatic Intelligence into Your Professional Life.* North Atlantic Books.

Tolle, Eckhart (2001). *The Power of Now: A Guide to Spiritual Enlightenment.* Yellow Kite.

Treleaven, David A. and Britton, Willoughby (2018). *Trauma-Sensitive Mindfulness: Practices for Safe and Transformative Healing.* W. W. Norton & Company.

van der Kolk, Bessel (1999). *Traumatic Stress: The Effects of Overwhelming Experience on Mind, Body and Society.* Guilford Press.

van der Kolk, Bessel (2015). *The Body Keeps the Score: Brain, Mind, and Body in the Healing of Trauma.* Penguin.

Weiser-Cornell, Ann (2013). *Focusing in Clinical Practice: the Essence of Change.* W. W. Norton & Company.

Weiser-Cornell, Ann (2015). *Presence: A Guide to Transforming Your Most Challenging Emotions.* Calluna Press.

Williamson, Marianne (2015). *A Return to Love; Reflections on the Principles of a Course in Miracles.* Harper Thorsons.